What Quee. ... aw:

Roderick Maclean and the Trial of Lunatics Act, 1883

What Queen Victoria Saw:

Roderick Maclean and the Trial of Lunatics Act, 1883

Stephen White

Barry Rose Law Publishers

What Queen Victoria Saw:

Roderick Maclean and the Trial of Lunatics Act, 1883

Items from the Royal Archives, Windsor [hereinafter RA], are reproduced by gracious permission of Her Majesty Queen Elizabeth II. Items from the Gladstone Papers, British Library, are reproduced by kind permission of Mr C.A. Gladstone. Items from the Harcourt Papers, Bodleian Library, Oxford University, are reproduced by kind permission of Mrs E.A. Gascoigne. Crown-copyright material in the Public Record Office, London [hereinafter PRO], is reproduced by kind permission of the Controller of Her Majesty's Stationery Office. I am also indebted to the late Dr John Hamilton for permission to peruse the file on Maclean at Broadmoor Special Hospital.

ISBN 1 872328 13 X

Published by
Barry Rose Law Publishers Limited
Chichester, England

Contents

Foreword

I have lectured on the insanity defence for more years than I care to remember. During my lectures I have often given a brief account of some of the more important historical aspects of the defence. In doing so I have tended to focus on three landmark cases. The first is that of James Hadfield, whose acquittal for the attempted assassination of George III led to the enactment of the Criminal Lunatics Act of 1800. The second is, not unnaturally, that of Daniel MacNaghten, whose being found"not guilty by reason of insanity" resulted in the formulation of the famous McNaghten Rules which have been fundamental in shaping the development of the insanity defence not only in this country but also in many other common law jurisdictions. While both Hadfield and M'Naghten have been the subject of considerable historical studies, the same cannot be said for the third and final case which is that of Roderick Maclean. What I did know about Maclean's case was very little. I knew that he had shot at Queen Victoria while she was riding in her carriage and that on learning of his acquittal under the M'Naghten Rules, her Majesty was so upset that she demanded that the law be changed to a verdict of "guilty but insane". This was achieved in the Trial of Lunatics Act of 1883 and so it remained until it was changed back to its original form in the Criminal Procedure (Insanity) Act 1964. I knew little else about Roderick Maclean but would like to have known more. Having now read Stephen White's fascinating account of the case I am at long last fully acquainted with all the details, some of which are not without contemporary significance. In this little gem of a book the author takes us on an historical journey in which there is much to learn about the political background surrounding Maclean's case and how the change in the verdict prompted by Queen Victoria was greeted at that time. We should be indebted to Stephen White for not only filling a gap in historical knowledge but also for giving us a book which is as interesting in its content as it is readable in its style.

R.D. Mackay
Professor of Criminal Policy and Mental Health
School of Law, De Montfort University

Summer Bank Holiday 1999

Preface

The British Trial of Lunatics Act of 1883 changed the form of the special verdict of insanity in criminal trials from "not guilty on the ground of insanity" to "guilty but insane". The Act was passed after Roderick Maclean discharged a pistol close to Queen Victoria, was tried for treason, and was acquitted on the ground of insanity. The conventional account of the passing of the Act is that the Queen could not understand how Maclean could have been not guilty since she saw him fire the gun herself, insisted on the change in the law, and was humoured by a reluctant Government and Parliament. This book examines the origins of this account and reassesses it. It locates Maclean's trial and the passing of the Act against the background of three features of the time: first, anarchism and the British tradition of harbouring exiles from Europe, secondly, unrest and political developments in Ireland, and thirdly, the Queen's dislike for both the person and the policies of her Prime Minister, Gladstone, and her mourning for her former Prime Minister, Disraeli, on the first anniversary of whose death Maclean's trial took place.

The book also examines the incomprehension and ridicule with which the Act was received by judges and doctors at the time and demonstrates the continued relevance of its history despite the special verdict being changed once more, in 1964, to "not guilty by reason of insanity".

Acts

Cases Cited

DPP v. Harper, [1997] 1 WLR 1406; 38 BMLR 91; [1997] RTR 200, 72n

Earl of Lonsdale v. Yates, 11 QBD 750 (1883), 71n

Yates v. The Queen, 14 QBD 648 at 655 (1884), 72n

R. v. Bernard, 2 Judicial Society 67 (1858-1863), 15n

R. v. Felstead, [1914] AC 534 68n

R. v. Hamilton, 7 St.Tr.N.S. 1130 (1848-50), 43n

R. v. Hill, 7 Cr.App.R 26 and 83 (1911), 68n

R. v. Horseferry Road Magistrates' Court, *ex parte* K, [1996] 3 All ER 719, 72n

R. v. Ireland, [1910] 1 KB 54 68n

R. v. Labouchere, [1884] 12 QBD 320, 70n

R. v. Law and Parnell, 14 Cox. C.C. 474, 505 and 508 (1880), 18n

R. v. Machardy [1911] 2 KB 1144 68n

R. v. Most, 7 QBD 244 (1881), 19n

R. v. Oxford, 9 Car. & P. 525 at 549, 173 ER 941 at 951 (1840), 5n

R. v. Pate, 8 St.Tr.N.S. 2 (1850-58), 43n, 45n

R. v. Taylor, [1915] 2 KB 709, 68n

Parliamentary Publications

Introduction

The Trial of Lunatics Act, 1883, was one of two Acts passed during Queen Victoria's reign as a result of treasonable activities consisting of attempted assaults on the person of the Queen. It altered the form of the special verdict which the Criminal Lunatics Act of 1800 had first required a jury to return upon defendants found to be insane from "not guilty on the ground of insanity" to "guilty but insane". It also restated the requirement that those absolved from responsibility because of insanity be automatically and indefinitely confined. The change to the form of the verdict survived until 1964, when the Criminal Procedure (Insanity) Act altered it again to "not guilty by reason of insanity". The automatic confinement of the criminally insane lasted until 1991, when the Criminal Procedure (Insanity and Unfitness to Plead) Act was passed to permit a few other methods of disposal, in addition to indefinite confinement, in cases where the penalty for a convicted offender is discretionary (in effect any offence except treason and murder).

The other Act was the Treason Act of 1842. This had been passed to avoid having to treat as traitors those who brandished firearms or discharged blanks in Queen Victoria's presence or vicinity, or who struck her or threw things at her.[1] The maximum penalty for an offence under the Act was seven years' transportation (eventually seven years' penal servitude after the ending of transportation) or three years'

1. Moran, "The Punitive Uses of the Insanity Defence: The Trial for Treason of Edward Oxford (1840)" 9 *International Journal of Law and Psychiatry* 171 (1986).

imprisonment with hard labour and a whipping.[2]

When the 1883 Act was released upon the world, neither doctors nor lawyers knew what to make of it. In the medical press it was completely ignored by the two journals that would be most expected to notice it, namely the *Journal of Mental Science*, the organ of the medical superintendents of asylums, and the *Journal of Psychological Medicine and Mental Pathology*,[3] then being edited by Lyttleton Forbes Winslow, the son of the doctor who had been called from the well of the court in 1843 to pronounce upon the sanity of Daniel M'Naughten without having interviewed him. *The Lancet*, to dispel some "misapprehensions" about the Act, observed that it had no practical effect except to simplify "the legal process of disposing of a well recognised set of cases": it did not explain what the misapprehensions were or wherein lay the simplification.[4] *The Medical Times and Gazette*, which argued that there were several important reforms that could be made to the law, such as the introduction of court appointed medical experts, was exceptional in the attention it bestowed on the Act and made it the occasion for some ponderous sarcasm:

---

2. There have probably been no more than seven prosecutions under the Act, the most recent being against Marcus Sarjeant, who was sentenced to five years' imprisonment in 1981 after discharging six blank cartridges at the Queen from a replica gun during the Trooping the Colour, *The Times* (London), Sept. 15, 1981, at 1, col. a, at 1, col. g, and 30, col. a; and Berlins, "Queen Victoria Incident led to Treason Act", *The Times* (London), June 15, 1981, at 3, col. a.
3. Shepherd, "Psychiatric Journals and the Evolution of Psychological Medicine," in W. Bynum, S. Lock and R. Porter (eds), *Medical Journals and Medical Knowledge: Historical Essays*, 188-206 at 190-193 (1992).
4. "Trial of Lunatics Bill", *The Lancet*, ii, 245, (Aug. 11, 1883).

> "To put in motion the cumbrous machinery of legislation, and to pass an Act of Parliament, for the sole purpose of altering one form of words for another form of words having virtually the same meaning and exactly the same practical effect, is a proceeding at which the non-legal mind may well be amazed. During a session which is so blocked with an excess of legislative business that the Government have again and again lamented their inability to pass measures of the utmost importance, and have denounced in the strongest possible terms the 'veiled obstruction' which they say has prevented them ... the Lord Chancellor can find time to bring in a Bill of four-hundred-and-twenty words for the purpose of substituting three words for seven! It is not as though there is no other means of effecting this important reform ... the alteration in the wording of a verdict [is] a matter of such petty detail that it might well be relegated to some sub-clause of [the] Criminal Code Bill. But the highest legal authority in the United Kingdom thinks otherwise. The defect which hurts no one is too important; the reform that has slumbered for generations is too urgent to wait for the general revision of the Criminal Code! It must be done instantly; it must have an Act to itself! Who can say after this that the Government is indifferent to the reform of the lunacy law?"[5]

In fact the measure had been rescued from a Criminal Code Bill which had been abandoned some seven weeks before.[6]

---

5. "Lunacy Law Reform", *Medical Times and Gazette*, ii, 182 (Aug. 18, 1883).
6. See *infra* p.67.

As for the lawyers, the Act came into effect immediately on receiving the Royal Assent on 25 August 1883 and was first applied three weeks later at the Old Bailey - though almost by chance and not without difficulty - when Johanna Culverwell was tried for the murder of her five-week-old son. She had left him in a pan of water where he had drowned. She pleaded guilty but was persuaded to change her plea by the judge, Watkin Williams J, and was then assigned a dock brief. The prosecution produced evidence that she was insane within the M'Naughten Rules. At the time a correspondence had just started in *The Times* about the impossibility of procuring copies of newly passed Acts of Parliament until after they had become operative.[7] In summing up to the jury Williams J observed:

> "At the present time he was not aware of the reasons for the passing of the new Act. It was certainly a curious illustration of the way things were done in this country, for although it was his duty to go to the court and preside over the trial, it was only by the merest accident that the fact that such an Act had been passed was made known to him, and he became aware of it by reading it in a newspaper. A copy of the Act was not delivered to him and he had to send to the Queen's printers to obtain one. He thought it was a most extraordinary thing."

Whether it was the Act or his not being told of it that

---

7. *The Times* (London), Sept. 13, 1883, at 7, col. d.

Williams found extraordinary is unclear but certainly he did not see the necessity for it. The former verdict of "not guilty on the ground of insanity" was a "correct, logical and legal verdict" and he observed that in parts the new Act was not "so clear and simple as those who passed it might have imagined". The wording of the Criminal Lunatics Act of 1800 had allowed the Attorney-General to argue at the trial of Edward Oxford for high treason in 1840, that a defendant insane at the time of the alleged offence could be indefinitely detained under the Act even though it had not been proved that he had done the act.[8] The new Act made it clear that this was not permissible. It applied where a person was "charged with an act or omission as a offence" and the jury found that he or she had done the act or made the omission but was not legally responsible because of insanity at the time. The jury were to return a verdict that the person "was guilty of the act or omission charged against him" but was insane. The problem arose because, in Williams J's view, the indictment did not charge Culverwell with any "act" such as putting the baby in the pan and drowning him: it charged her simply with killing and murdering him. After legal argument about

8. *R. v. Oxford*, 9 Car. & P. 525 at 549, 173 ER 941 at 951 (1840). The 1800 Act provided that where evidence of insanity was given at a person's trial for treason "the jury shall be required to find specially whether such person was insane at the time of the commission of the offence, and to declare whether such person was acquitted by them on account of such insanity; and if they shall find that such person was insane ..., the court shall order such person to be kept in strict custody ... until His Majesty's pleasure be known". There is an account of the trial and argument in White, "Acts and Facts", 62 *Journal of Criminal Law* 360 at 366 (1998). Oxford, like Maclean, had discharged a pistol in the vicinity of the Queen but it was unclear with what, if anything, it was charged.

what "the act" was, the jury reported that "we find the prisoner guilty, but that she was insane at the time, she committed the act". Williams J refused to accept a verdict that she was guilty of murder. After further legal argument the jury returned another verdict, which the judge did accept: "the prisoner was guilty of the act of killing the child by immersing it in the pan of water and suffocating it, but that at the time she did so she was insane and not responsible for her actions".[9] *The Law Times*, which had earlier welcomed the Act as likely to prove "of considerable practical value" without saying how, now joined in Williams J's strictures on its "absurdity".[10] *The Law Journal* agreed and added that "the most perverse ingenuity" could not have devised a more unfortunate title for an Act since it might lead students of the law to think that "in this country lunatics are treated as capable of committing a crime, and, consequently, as liable to the usual consequences of crime".[11] This was, as will be seen, exactly what Queen Victoria intended lunatics should think. Two days after Culverwell's trial another judge was completely taken by surprise at the Old Bailey during the trial of William Gouldstone for the murder of his children. Day J had been unaware of the Act until prosecuting counsel had handed him a copy. He too impliedly criticised the illogicality of the new verdict but any final decision about its correct form was rendered unnecessary when the jury

---

9. *The Times* (London), Sept. 13, 1883, at 10, col. a, and "Mr. Justice Williams and the Trial of Lunatics Act", 18 *Law Journal* 501 (Sept. 15, 1883). See too the puzzled note about the Act in "Current Topics", 27 *Solicitors' Journal* 733 (Sept. 15, 1883).
10. 75 *Law Times* 331 and 339 (Sept. 1 and 15, 1883).
11. 18 *Law Journal* 494 (Sept. 15, 1883).

convicted Gouldstone.[12] A month later, at the trial of James Cole, Denman J lined up with Williams and Day JJ: he was "not inclined to disagree with" their criticisms of the Act.[13]

12. *The Times* (London), Sept. 15, 1883, at 12, col. a. The medical press were extremely critical about the way the medical evidence had been dealt with at the trial and Gouldstone's sentence was commuted, see *The Lancet* ii, 505, 520 and 604 (Sept. 22 and Oct. 6, 1883), *British Medical Journal*, ii, 583, 639 and 682 (Sept. 22 and 29 and Oct. 6, 1883), and 29 *Journal of Mental Science* 534-612 (1883). The case provides an example, startling to modern English eyes, of the jurymen engaging in correspondence about the case in the press, see the letters from "One of the Jury" and "The Foreman of the Jury", *Daily Telegraph* (London), Sept. 17, 1883, at 3, col. d and Sept. 19, 1883, at 3, col. f.
13. *The Times* (London), Oct. 19, 1883, at 8, col. a.

What Queen Victoria Saw

The 1883 Act was passed after Roderick Maclean had been tried and acquitted of high treason on the ground of insanity. He had discharged a pistol in the vicinity of Queen Victoria as she was being driven away from the railway station to the Castle at Windsor.

A story, frequently repeated in accounts of the genesis of the Act,[14] is that on learning of the verdict Victoria exclaimed "how can he be not guilty? I saw him fire the gun myself" - or words to that effect - and insisted on a change in the law. This is a part-truth and, disappointingly, the part which is untrue is the best part of it.

Victoria did not see Maclean fire at her. The best evidence for saying so comes from the Journal of the Queen herself. Her entry for 2 March records that she heard the shot but thought it was an explosion from the engine at the station and did not realise that it might have been a shot intended for her until she noticed Maclean being manhandled by the crowd. Commenting on a photo of Maclean she wrote:

> "It is a horrid, cruel face - wh. she is glad she did not see."[15]

Indeed she made the point that she was far less alarmed by the incident than she had been by O'Connor's far less

---

14. R. Partridge, *Broadmoor: A History of Criminal Lunacy and Its Problems*, 5 (1953), Morris, "Daniel M'Naughten and the Death Penalty", 6 *Res Judicatae* 304 at 311 (1953), F. Whitlock, *Criminal Responsibility and Mental Illness*, 43 (1963), and S. Glueck, *Law and Psychiatry: Cold War or Entente Cordiale?*, 35 (1967).
15. Letter from the Queen, (Mar, undated, 1882), RA L14/115.

dangerous assault 10 years' previously, which she had been aware of as it was made.[16]

Other contemporary evidence, if more be needed, confirms Victoria's account. The telegram Sir Henry Ponsonby, the Queen's Private Secretary, sent to the Prime Minister, Mr Gladstone, informing him of the incident stated that:

> "Queen was not alarmed did not see the act though Princess Beatrice did."[17]

On the day after the incident, when Vernon Harcourt, the Home Secretary, travelled from London to Windsor to attend the Queen, Lewis Harcourt recorded in his journal that his father

> "returned at 2 and gave a good account of her; she was not the least upset for she had luckily received no shock as she did not actually see the man shoot and of course there is a wide difference between seeing a man aim and fire at you and being told subsequently that a man has shot at you. She very naively said 'I heard a report, but took no notice of it till I saw a man being arrested and then I began to think that the shot was meant for me'."[18]

---

16. RA Queen Victoria's Journal, (Mar. 2, 1882), reprinted in 3 *The Letters of Queen Victoria* [Second series]: *A Selection from Her Majesty's Correspondence and Journals Between the Years 1862 and 1885*, 265 (G. Buckle ed. 1928). On the O'Connor case see *infra* p.43 and n.127.
17. 2 P. Guedalla, *The Queen and Mr Gladstone, 1880-1898*, 181[835] (1933).
18. *Journal of Lewis Harcourt*, (Mar. 3, 1882), MS. Harcourt dep. 350, at f.49, Bodleain Library, Oxford University.

Whether Victoria could have seen Maclean is another matter, about which it is not possible to be sure. The evidence, as reported in the newspapers, of who was in the Queen's carriage and where they were sitting is not completely consistent but it is certain that the carriage had three occupants, the Queen, Princess Beatrice, the Queen's youngest daughter, and the Duchess of Roxburghe, the Queen's lady in waiting, who had entered it in that order from its left. The better view seems to be that the Queen and Princess Beatrice were sitting alongside each other facing forward, with the Queen on the right, and the Duchess was sitting opposite them with her back to the horses. The window of the door through which they had entered was down and Maclean was slightly in front of, and about 15 yards from, the carriage on that side when he fired. Princess Beatrice did see Maclean fire and it is therefore likely that Victoria would have been in Maclean's line of vision. However, Maclean always denied having aimed at anyone and in an undated letter written in Broadmoor, apparently for public release, in which he admitted seeing Princess Beatrice, he wrote that he could not have aimed at the Queen because from where he was standing he could not see her and that "if her Majesty herself were questioned she would admit that from her seat she did not see me".[19]

As Professor Walker has pointed out, the person who seems to have first printed the story that Victoria saw

19. The letter was bought by the Department of the History of Medicine, University of Kansas, sometime before 1959, Letter from L.R.C. Agnew, (May 28, 1959), File No. 1095 on Roderick Maclean, Broadmoor Special Hospital.

Maclean fire is Lytton Strachey. In his biography of the Queen, Strachey wrote:

> "Victoria ... was very much annoyed. What did the jury mean, she asked, by saying that Maclean was not guilty? It was perfectly clear that he was guilty - she had seen him fire off the pistol herself."[20]

Two features of Strachey's novel approach to writing biography were his adoption of a "point of view" about his subjects and the use of the well chosen quotation to reveal his subject's true selves.[21] Strachey was convinced that it was through their own words that people disclosed their real character. This approach inevitably made his work vulnerable to charges of historical inaccuracy and, although Strachey's canon of biography included "truth to the facts", there is no doubt that some of his biographical studies are flawed in this respect. But, according to Sanders, the literary critic, his study of Queen Victoria belongs to the group of studies that have been least criticised on this account.[22] On this matter of whether Victoria saw Maclean fire at her, however, he was indubitably wrong.

Strachey based his biographical studies on published sources only. He had completed almost all his research for Queen Victoria by April 1920 and he completed the book

---

20. L. Strachey, *Queen Victoria*, 278 (1921).
21. C. Sanders, *Lytton Strachey: His Mind and Art*, 232 & 316-319 (1957).
22. *Id.*, at 203; and 2 M. Holroyd, *Lytton Strachey: A Critical Biography: The Years of Achievement* (1910-1932), 407 (1968). Holroyd's critique of Strachey's *Queen Victoria* is curtailed in later, revised versions of his biography of Strachey.

itself in late January 1921.[23] At this time only the first series of Queen Victoria's letters, covering the first 24 years of her reign, had been issued: the second, covering the years 1882 and 1883 among others, was not published until 1928 and the Gladstone family's corrective to the impression conveyed by these not until 1933.[24]

On 15 December 1920, *The Times* published a letter from Herbert Stephen, who had entered into a controversy about insanity and crime. Part of it ran:

> "It may conduce to a better understanding of that Act and the verdict 'guilty but insane' ... if I may make public for the first time, the reason why that Act was passed. In 1882 a lunatic fired a pistol at Queen Victoria. He was tried for high treason, and found not guilty on the ground of insanity. The form of the verdict displeased the Queen ... (She) maintained that whether or not the man was guilty of high treason, he was guilty of firing a pistol at her. She said that the verdict in such cases ought to begin not with the words Not Guilty but with the word Guilty. Her constitutional advisers did not agree with her view but could not persuade her to accept theirs. They therefore explained to the leaders of the opposite party the real reason of their proposal to alter the verdict, and the Act of 1883 was passed without controversy ... My opinion is

---

23. *Id.*, at 278, 377, and 386-391. This presumably explains the reference in a letter the painter Dora Carrington sent Strachey in December 1920. Under a sketch of him lying in a bowl of soup and reading a book she wrote "Last Night I Dreamt of Queen Victoria", see D. Garnet, *Carrington: Letters and Extracts from Her Diaries* 171, (1970).

24. 3 Buckle *supra* n. 16; 2 Guedalla *supra* n. 17.

that the Act of 1883 ought not to have been passed and would not have been passed if the occurrence which led to it had taken place during the Premiership of Lord Beaconsfield and the Chancellorship of Lord Cairns ..."[25]

Herbert Stephen was in a position to know how the Act had come to be passed because his father, James Fitzjames Stephen, was one of the committee of three judges who were consulted over the form the legislation should take. The close involvement of the Stephen family in Strachey's Bloomsbury Circle makes it quite possible that Strachey had discussed the history of the Act with Herbert Stephen.

Although Stephen's letter is true in outline, there is more to the passing of the Act than it reveals. The three features of the time that explain the Act's passage are, first, anarchism and the British tradition of harbouring political exiles from Europe, secondly, events in Ireland, and, thirdly, as Stephen's letter hints, Victoria's political allegiance and her increasingly strained personal relationship with Gladstone.

---

25. Stephen, "Insanity and Crime", *The Times* (London), Dec. 15, 1920, at 8, col. a.

Stained glass window commemorating Queen Victoria's escape from injury by Maclean, St Michael and All Angels, Hughenden, Bucks

Reproduced with the kind permission of the Vicar and Churchwarden of St Michael and All Angels, Hughenden, Bucks

Queen Victoria's Memorial to Benjamin Disraeli St Michael and All Angels, Hughenden, Bucks

The Disraeli Family tomb, St Michael and All Angels, Hughenden, Bucks

The Political Background

In the third-quarter of the nineteenth century Britons of all classes prided themselves on being citizens of a country free of the threat of terrorist violence. Indeed, to the chagrin of her neighbours, Britain harboured agitators exiled from the continent without being at all apprehensive that their machinations would be directed against her.[26] Free and democratic institutions, Britons claimed, so notably lacking in the countries from which the exiles came, rendered (mainland) Britain immune to subversion. It was fortunate they thought so because those very institutions were inimical to the methods of policing that would be resorted to should subversion become a threat: since the steam had gone out of Chartism with the failure of the second National Petition in April 1848 mainland Britain had had virtually no secret or political police.[27]

An indication of the public temper in the mid-century is provided by the Orsini affair. Felice Orsini was an Italian revolutionary living in London who felt that the Emperor Napoleon III was hindering the movement towards Italian independence. In 1858, he and three other Italians who had also lived in England, attempted to assassinate Napoleon outside the Paris Opera in accordance with a plan hatched

---

26. J. Quail, *The Slow Burning Fuse: The Lost History of the British Anarchists* (1978); H. Oliver, *The International Anarchist Movement in Late Victorian London* (1983).
27. For four months after the bombing of Clerkenwell prison by Fenians in December 1867 the Government had a secret intelligence organisation operating outside the Metropolitan Police, see Smith, "The Police and the Fenians" in P. Smith, *Policing Victorian London: Political Policing, Public Order and the London Metropolitan Police*, 193-195 (1985).

in London and with a bomb made to order in Birmingham. Napoleon escaped injury, but 10 people were killed and many others injured. In the immediate wake of the attempt, Palmerston, the Prime Minister, introduced a bill to criminalise conspiracies in this country to commit murder abroad. It was known, however, that the French had protested about the immunity such conspirators enjoyed. The measure was seen as kowtowing to France. The bill was defeated, and Palmerston's administration brought down. As ss.4 and 5 of the Offences against the Person Act, 1861, the measure was eventually accepted during Palmerston's second administration. But it was a less stringent one, and the unwisdom of prosecutions after 1858 was confirmed by the acquittal by an Old Bailey jury of Simon Bernard, a French refugee living in London, in the face of the clearest evidence that he had been an accessory to the murders committed by Orsini.

This climate of thought also protected aliens while the review that led to the Extradition Act of 1870 was being undertaken.[28] By 1880, however, things were beginning to change.[29]

---

28. B. Porter, *The Refugee Question in Mid-Victorian Politics,* 170, 206 and 211 (1979); Hearder, "Napoleon III's Threat to break off Diplomatic Relations with England during the Crisis over the Orsini Attempt in 1858", 72 *English Historical Review* 474 (1957); Woodall, "Orsini and the Fall of Palmerston", *History Today* 636 (1976); *R. v. Bernard,* 8 St. Tr. N.S. 887 (1850-1858); Stephen, "Assassination Abroad and Complicity at Home: On the Point of Law involved in the Case of *Reg. v. Bernard*", 2 *Judicial Society* 67 (1858-1863).

29. Porter *supra* n.28; Porter, "The British Government and Political Refugees, c. 1880-1914", 2 *Immigrants and Minorities,* 23 (1983) reprinted in J. Slatter (ed.), *From the Other Shore: Russian Political Emigrants in Britain, 1880-1917,*

In March 1880 Disraeli called a general election and tried to make Irish Home Rule its central issue. Unprotestingly lured from retirement by the eclat of capturing a seat which since 1841 had been Whig or Liberal held for only six years, Gladstone had embarked, in the previous November, on the fortnight of sustained oratory that was his unprecedented Midlothian campaign. From Chester to Aberfeldy, from the verandah of his pullman railway carriage, at stations, in halls and the open air, by day and torch-light night he indicted[30] Disraeli's government to large audiences, not always spontaneously assembled. He criticised the Government's foreign and imperial policy particularly. When the election was called he gave an encore.[31] Against most expectations the

---

23 (1984); B. Porter, *Plots and Paranoia: A History of Political Espionage in Britain* (1989); Porter, "'Bureau and Barrack': Early Victorian Attitudes towards the Continent", 27 *Victorian Studies* 407 (1984).

30. Gladstone set out the heads of the indictment from the very start in his letter, printed in *The Times* (London), Feb. 2, 1879, at 10, col. c, accepting the Midlothian Liberal Association's invitation to stand as their Parliamentary candidate. He sustained the forensic metaphor, with the nation as jury, throughout his campaign but it was especially prominent in his first Midlothian speech at Edinburgh, 25 November 1879, his speech at Perth Railway station 1 December 1879, and his speech at West Calder, 2 April 1880. The West Calder speech was printed in *The Times* (London), Apr. 3, 1880, at 8, col. f.

31. W. Gladstone, *Political Speeches in Scotland, November and December* 1879 (1879) reprinted with an introduction by M.R.D. Foot as *Midlothian Speeches* 1879 (1971); W. Gladstone, *Political Speeches in Scotland, March and April 1880* (1880); Kelley, "Midlothian: A Study in Ideas and Politics", 4 *Victorian Studies* 119 (1961); J. Morley, *The Life of William Ewart Gladstone (1872-1898)*, 192 (1907); R. James, *Rosebery: A Biography of Archibald Philip, Fifth Earl of Rosebery*, 91 (1963); J. Marlow, *Mr & Mrs Gladstone: An Intimate Biography*, 190 (1977); Brooks, "Gladstone and Midlothian: The Background to the First Campaign", 64 *Scottish Historical Review* 42 (1985).

Liberals won - and with a large overall majority - and, despite the contribution of Joseph Chamberlain's newly created national Liberal Federation to the victory,[32] Gladstone's was the credit. During the six years of Disraeli's government, however, Queen Victoria's attitude to Gladstone had changed and his recent demagoguery, as she thought of it, had appalled her. Before the election she had declared that she would never accept him again as a Minister, let alone a Prime Minister, and after it she threatened to abdicate rather than commission him to form a government. Nevertheless, when told that Gladstone had to be in the Cabinet and would not serve under either Lord Granville, who had been leading the Liberal party since Gladstone's resignation in 1875, or Lord Hartington, the party's leader in the House of Commons, she summoned him (as she was to have to do twice more).[32a]

Gladstone's government turned out to be far less powerful than the size of its majority would suggest. The Liberal Party was split over how Ireland should be ruled, as over other issues, and it faced an opposition composed not only of

---

32. Roy Jenkins *Gladstone,* 412 and 441 (1995).

32a. E. Longford, *Victoria, R.I.,* 356-542 (1964); Rossi, "Home Rule and the Liverpool By-Election of 1880", 19 *Irish Historical Studies* 156 (1974-75); T. Lloyd, *The General Election of 1880* (1968); Jenkins, "Gladstone, The Whigs and Leadership of the Liberal Party, 1879-1880", 27 *Historical Journal* 337 (1984); T. Jenkins, *Gladstone, Whigery and the Liberal Party, 1874-1886,* (1988); 9 *The Gladstone Diaries with Cabinet Minutes and Prime-Ministerial Correspondence, January 1875-December 1880,* xxiii-xxvii, xxxii-xxxvii, and xlvii-lxxiii (H. Matthew ed. 1986); W. Hancock (Ed.), *English Historical Documents 1874-1914,* 27-32 (1977); The Queen to Sir Henry Ponsonby (Apr. 4, 1880) in A. Ponsonby, *Henry Ponsonby: Queen Victoria's Private Secretary: His Life From His Letters,* 184 (1942).

defeated Tories but of a group of some 65 obstructive Irish nationalist members led by Charles Stewart Parnell.[33] Preferring to rely on the ordinary resources of the law, Gladstone allowed the Irish Coercion Act to lapse and promoted a Land Bill to allow tenants in Ireland a measure of compensation for eviction. This would not have been Victoria's way who was for coercion first.[34] The rejection of the Land Bill by the Lords in August was followed by renewed violence in Ireland, the institution of "boycotting",[35] and the prosecution of Parnell in Dublin for conspiracy. But the prosecution failed on January 25, 1881.[36] In anticipation of this, a new Coercion Bill had been introduced. Virtually isolated in his opposition to the bill, Gladstone had agreed to support it in return for a substantial new Land Bill which, as finally settled, gave tenants the right to a fair rent judicially determined, fixity of tenure, and freedom to sell their interests in the land. The Coercion Bill, which reintroduced internment, was passed on March 2, 1882 and the Land Bill, introduced five weeks later, was passed on August 22, 1882.[37]

---

33. Thorley, "The Irish Home Rule Party and Parliamentary Obstruction, 1874-87", 12 *Irish Historical Studies* 38 (1960).
34. Longford, *supra* n. 32a, at 555 and 559; Letters from the Queen to Gladstone, (Nov. 22, Dec. 23, and Dec. 26, 1880), reprinted in 2 Guedalla *supra* n.17, at 124[710], 126[714] and 127[716].
35. J. Marlow, *Captain Boycott and the Irish* (1973).
36. *R. v. Law and Parnell*, 14 Cox. C.C. 474, 505 and 508 (1880).
37. J. Hammond, *Gladstone and the Irish Nation*, 163-283 (1964); R. Kee, *The Laurel and the Ivy: The Story of Charles Stewart Parnell and Irish Nationalism*, 224-446 (1994); T. Corfe, *The Phoenix Park Murders: Conflict, Compromise and Tragedy in Ireland, 1879-1882*, 72-180 (1968); Hawkins, "Gladstone, Forster, and the Release of Parnell, 1882-8", 5 *Irish Historical Studies* 417 (1969); Cooke and

The result of the coercive measures was the start of a bombing campaign on the mainland, orchestrated by American Fenians. In the first half of 1881 there were three Fenian bomb explosions on the mainland - at Salford and Chester barracks and Liverpool Town Hall - and one foiled one at the Mansion House in London.[38] The changing nature and context of terrorist activity was marked by the prosecution in May 1881 of Johann Most, a German exile, for publishing in *Der Freiheit*, his anarchist newssheet, a piece exulting in the assassination of Tsar Alexander II and advocating the murder of a monarch a month.[39] The prosecution served two purposes. It was a sop to European governments who were pressing for harsher measures against exiles in Britain and seeking an international conference to co-ordinate measures against terrorism as a

---

Vincent, "Herbert Gladstone, Forster, and Northern Ireland, 1881-82", 17 *Irish Historical Studies* 521 (1971) and 18 *Irish Historical Studies* 74 (1972); Warren, "Forster, the Liberals and New Directions in Irish Policy 1880-82", 6 *Parliamentary History* 95 (1987); 2 T. Wemyss Reid, *Life of the Right Honourable William Edward Forster*, 233 (1888); 1 *The Diary of Sir Edward Walter Hamilton 1880-1885*, 73-161 *passim* (D. Bahlman ed. (1972); Matthew, *supra* n. 32a, lxxiii-lxxix; 10 *The Gladstone Diaries with Cabinet Minutes and Prime-Ministerial Correspondence*, January *1881-June 1883*, cx-cxx (H. Matthew ed. 1990).

38. K. Short, *The Dynamite War: Irish-American Bombers in Victorian London* (1979); *R. v. Gallagher, Whitehead, Wilson, Ansburgh, and Curtin*, 15 Cox C.C. 291 (1883). W. D'Arcy, *The Fenian Movement in the United States: 1858-1886*, 400-406 (1947) does not refer to these explosions.

39. Porter, "The Freiheit Prosecutions, 1881-82", 23 *Historical Journal* 833 (1980); B. Porter, *The Origins of the Vigilant State: The London Metropolitan Police Special Branch Before The First World War* (1987); B. Porter, *The Origins of Britain's Political Police*, (Warwick Working Papers in Social History No. 3, 1985); Porter, "Secrecy and the Special Branch, 1880-1914", 52(1) *Bulletin for the Study of Labour History* 8 (1987); and *R. v. Most*, 7 QBD 244 (1881).

means of securing this. It also made it easier for the Government to ask for action to be taken against Fenians in America.[40] The killing of President Garfield by Charles Guiteau in July 1881[41] was a warning that even republicanism was no sure prophylactic for assassination. The Queen, when travelling by rail, began to be preceded by a dummy royal train.[42] With Parnell's restraining influence removed in October by his internment secret Fenian societies burgeoned.[43]

Thus, when in the following year Roderick Maclean discharged a revolver, apparently at Queen Victoria, as she drove away in a closed landau from the railway station to the Castle at Windsor, people wondered anxiously whether the incident was different from the alarming but mostly harmless attacks to which the Queen had previously been subjected.[44] "He may prove the first of the English nihilists", wrote the *Daily Telegraph*.[45] In one important and worrying respect the incident was different from all but the earliest attacks:[46]

---

40. *Correspondence respecting the Publication in the United States of Incitements to Outrages in England*, C. 3194, (HC Papers, 1882, v. 80, 53); Edwards, "American Diplomats and Irish Coercion, 1880-1883", 1 *Journal of American Studies* 213 (1967).
41. C. Rosenberg, *The Trial of the Assassin Guiteau: Psychiatry and Law in the Guilded Age* (1968). Guiteau, whose trial lasted from 14 November 1881 to 5 January 1882, was not executed until 30 June 1882.
42. B. Porter, 1987, *supra* n. 39, 26.
43. F. Lyons, *Charles Stewart Parnell*, 177 (1977).
44. 1 N. Walker, *Crime and Insanity in England: The Historical Perspective*, 186-193 (1968); Walker, "1883 and All That: A Historical Note on the Criminal Procedure (Insanity) Act 1964 (c.84)", [1966] *Crim. L.R.* 17; Walker, "Queen Victoria was Right", (1963) *New Society* 15 (1963).
45. *The Daily Telegraph* (London) Mar. 3, 1882, at 6, col. h.
46. *Moran, supra* n.1.

Maclean's gun had been loaded with live ammunition.[47] It was because of this that the authorities prevaricated momentarily over whether to pursue a charge under the reasonably well tested Treason Act of 1842.

---

47. It was also different in another, minor, respect: it took place out of London. *The Morning Post* (as summarised in the *St James' Gazette*, Mar. 3, 182, at 12, col. b), commenting on the reclusiveness and absences from London for which Victoria was criticised, regretted that Maclean's attack might make her even more withdrawn. On Victoria's seclusiveness see too F. Hardie, *The Political Influence of Queen Victoria, 1861-1901* at 205 & 215 (1963).

Evidence of Mental Disorder at the Trial

The incident outside Windsor railway station took place at about 5.15 on the afternoon of Thursday March 2, 1882. By the time of the Maclean's trial, some seven weeks later, evidence of his derangement from an early age was overwhelming. In 1866 he had been treated for six weeks by a Dr Towers Smith for a severe wound to the head. Samuel Stanesby, a close family friend for the previous 20 years, with whom Maclean had lived in 1871 and who had seen him frequently since,[48] testified to Maclean's having had "fits", to "great peculiarities in his conduct", and to his own (Stanesby's belief) that Maclean was "absolutely insane". There was also evidence from a clergyman from Newton Valence in Hampshire, who had been in the crowd outside Windsor station. By an odd chance Maclean had collapsed outside his house during an epileptic seizure on 23 February, the day Maclean left Portsmouth to walk to Windsor.[49] In 1874 Henry Maudsley had certified Maclean as "not of perfectly sound mind". So had Dr Alfred Goodrich. Maudsley told the court that he believed that, though Maclean might have recovered, it was more probable that he would not. In June 1880 Maclean was certified by a Dr Charles Hitchins and admitted to the Bath and Somerset Lunatic Asylum, where he remained until July the following

48. Stanesby was an artist and is catalogued in C. Wood, *Dictionary of Victorian Painters*, 446 (1985) as having a short period of success between 1850 and 1853 and as having exhibited two portraits at a Royal Society of Artists Exhibition and a painting of fowls at the Royal Academy.

49. The record forwarded with Maclean when he was transferred from Reading Gaol to Broadmoor recorded that he was not suffering from epilepsy, File No. 1095 *supra* n. 19.

year. Dr Thomas Sheldon, an assistant medical attendant at the asylum, testified that he suffered from delusions, melancholia and homicidal mania. Sheldon told the court that, although Maclean had recovered by the time of his discharge, he had thought it likely that Maclean's disorder would recur and that he would need to be reconfined. Stanesby was able to confirm that three letters produced by the defence had been written by Maclean. Two of them had been written just before Maclean's admission to Wells Asylum and spoke of his paranoia and his intention to be revenged:

> "... I can hardly contain myself in fact. I mean, if they don't cease wearing blue, I will commit murder. In fact, I could not prevent myself committing murder about them not assisting me to get a letter from the Sanatorium, and yet they have the audacity to wear blue ... I really think I cannot prevent myself having revenge on the English people ... I fear it will be just as bad in Boulogne or elsewhere. What chances have I to cope with the millions of people who are against me? ... I intend to carry my determination into effect today (Monday), and after it's done, I shall write you a letter. Of course I shall not remove nor give myself up, but doubtless they will take me into custody the next day. If I cannot commit murder (I really assure you, Annie, I mean what I write) in one way, I will in another way. All I can add is, if there is more difficulty, there may be more victims ... I have written a confession, which I intend to give to the superintendent. If they will not read it in court, will you try and persuade them to, as I wish the English people to know that they did

> not make such a fool of me as they supposed, and, as they previously were at enmity for nothing, how they shall be at enmity for something? Of course, you can see the confession is 'Why I committed murder', not about the museum affair ..."

There was also evidence from four doctors who had examined Maclean since his arrest. One, a Henry Manning of the Laverstock Asylum in Salisbury, had been instructed by Maclean's family, the other three, Edgar Sheppard, Professor of Psychology at King's College, London, and Medical Superintendent at Colney Hatch Asylum, William Orange, the Medical Superintendent of Broadmoor, and Oliver Maurice, the doctor at Reading Gaol, had been instructed by the Crown. They all gave their opinion that Maclean was insane. They testified to his continuing paranoia and fixation over people wearing blue, though to this was added a belief in the malevolence (or benevolence) towards him of any numeral containing the number four.[50]

---

50. "Trial of Maclean", *The Times* (London), Apr. 20, 1882, at 11, col. a. A slightly fuller account of the examination of the medical witnesses is given in "Attempt to Shoot the Queen", 28 *Journal of Mental Science* 307 (1882).

Biographical Details in the Press

In addition to this evidence, which was presented at his trial, other details of Maclean's life had been filled in by the press in the meantime. He had been born in London in 1854. He may have been an inmate of the Bedminster workhouse in Somerset in 1870.[51] He may have lived under the name of Roderigues Maclean in Jamaica.[52] He may have managed the Co-operative store at Weymouth.[53] (On his arrest he had described himself as a grocer's assistant, according to some accounts. According to others, he had said he was an unemployed clerk.) In 1874 he had been acquitted at the Kent Assizes of inciting a 12-year-old boy to derail a train.[54] Many newspaper readers learned that Wollaston Knocker, the Town Clerk of Dover, who had defended him, had written a "long letter giving an account of the prisoner's hallucinations and eccentricities previous to that date and the trouble he had been to his father and friends".[55] Readers of

---

51. *Reading Mercury*, Mar. 11, 1882, at 2, col. b.
52. *The Times* (London), Mar. 6, 1882, at 2, col. b; *Berkshire Chronicle*, Feb. 2, 1882, at 2, col. b.
53. *Sussex Daily News*, Mar. 4, 1882.
54. Reasonably full and very similar accounts of the committal proceedings are in the *Dover Express*, Aug. 21, 1874, the *Dover Chronicle and Kent and Sussex Advertiser*, Aug. 22, 1874, and the *Dover Standard*, Aug. 22, 1874, at 3, col. a. The fullest account of the trial is in the *Kent Messenger and Maidstone Telegraph*, Dec. 12, 1874. Shorter accounts are in the *Maidstone and Kentish Journal*, Dec. 12, 1874, at 3, the *South Eastern Gazette*, Dec. 12, 1874, at 2, col. e, the *Dover Chronicle and Kent and Sussex Advertiser*, Dec. 12, 1874, at 6, col. b. and the *Dover Standard*, Dec. 12, 1874, at 3, col. c. The case raised legal issues about impossibility in attempts and accessorial liability to a principal *doli incapax*.
55. *The Times* (London), Mar. 4, 1882, at 10, col. a; *Reading Mercury*, Mar. 11, 1882, at 2, col. b.

the *Windsor and Eton Express* and *Reynold's Newspaper*, which printed what appears to have been a large portion, if not all, of Wollaston Knocker's letter, learned that the hallucinations and eccentricities included the belief that a person in mourning garb, encountered in the street, was a harbinger of Maclean's imminent death and that, should Maclean live beyond a certain date, which was unlikely, he would be immortal. He had believed that sailors on a ship on which he had just embarked for America intended to murder him and that his father had made arrangements with the captain of the ship to which he was then transferred to cast him overboard. He had threatened to kill not only his father but other members of the family and had spoken of blowing up St Paul's Cathedral and Westminster Abbey.[56] Readers also learned that Maclean's father had told Knocker that Maclean had made two previous and undiscovered attempts to derail a train.[57]

In 1877 Maclean had been living in Guildford. He had sent a verse he had written to the Queen:

"On your thrown you set and rule us all,
By justice you make known
All your power, and the people like
To cheer the Queen they call their own,
When your lamented husband left us,
And went were troubles find no share,

---

56. *Windsor and Eton Express*, Mar. 11, 1882; *Reynold's Newspaper* (London), Mar. 12, 1882, at 1, col. c.
57. *Windsor and Eton Express*, Mar. 11, 1882

How we felt for you and tried too lessen
The sting of bad fate you had to bare,
But God knows whats for our best
Sent you comfort in your most trying hour,
And made you bare your troubles as a nobly
woman should,
And the people showed their love, and like
your power,
When History tells, of your reign,
They will think of you and say,
Its the Queen who made her people happy,
By affection and justice that how she rule
the sway."

The verse was returned by a lady in waiting because "the Queen never accepts manuscript poetry", and was produced by Maclean's landlady who had moved him on before it arrived.[58] Maclean had alarmed her by revealing he was carrying a dagger up his coat sleeve with which to "take care of himself" as he set out to visit a local fair.[59] He was thought to have lived in Shoreham, Sussex, between 1878 and 1880, where his eccentricities gave the local children much amusement. These included always carrying an open umbrella and calling himself the Prince of Wales.[60] He was

58. For this reason it is unlikely that Maclean's troubles sprang from this rejection of his verse as was suggested by Bayes, "The Bullet from his Gun (Bought in Portsmouth) Sped towards the Queen he Revered", *Evening News* (Portsmouth), Nov. 29, 1963, at 12.

59. *Surrey Advertiser*, Mar. 11, 1882, at 5, col. b.

60. *Sussex Advertiser*, Mar. 9, 1882.

identified as having emerged from Castle Yard at Windsor in the summer or autumn of 1881 and enquired where the Queen slept.[61]

61. *The Times* (London), Mar. 8, 1882, at 7, col. f; *Windsor and Eton Express*, Mar. 11, 1882; *Lloyd's Weekly Newspaper* (London), Mar. 12, 1882, at 12, col. b.

Events Leading up to the Shooting

In the weeks immediately before the incident at Windsor Maclean had been in the Brighton and Steyning Union workhouse in Shoreham,[62] whence he had walked to Portsmouth.[63] He had arrived in Portsmouth on 9 February, claiming to have been sent there as reporter for a Sussex newspaper. (Several accounts speak of his good education and ability to speak at least two foreign languages fluently, French and German; he was reported to have written poetry for a West Surrey newspaper;[64] and among the possessions found on him on his arrest was a page on which was written "The Fourth Path, a novel by Roderick Maclean. Four drops of sweet nitre and half a tumbler of Water".[65]) He also claimed that his father had been a proprietor of *Fun*[66] and had

---

62. There was also a report of his having been turned away, cursing the Queen, from the infirmary in Walworth Road, Southwark, *The Times* (London), Mar. 4, 1882, at 1, col. b.
63. *Brighton Gazette,* Mar. 4, 1882.
64. *Daily News* (London), Mar. 4, 1882, at 5, col. f.
65. *Brighton Gazette,* Mar. 4, 1882. "The Fourth Oath" according the *Evening News* (Portsmouth), Apr. 3, 1882.
66. A Charles Maclean was the founder and first proprietor of *Fun* (from 1861 to 1865) which was published by his son, also named Charles, see Steadman, "Fun" in Alvin Sullivan (ed.), *British Literary Magazines: The Victorian and Edwardian Age 1837-1913,* 135-138 (1984); Frederic Boase, *Modern English Biography*, vol.2, 648 (1897); and Edward S. Lauterbach, *"Fun" and its Contributors: the Literary History of Victorian Humour Magazine,* Ph.D. dissertation, University of Illinois, 4-11 (1961). One of Roderick Maclean's brothers was called Charles, but I have not found an entry for Roderick's birth (which would have given his father's name) in the General Register Office's indexes to registrations of births for the years 1853 to 1856 inclusive. The Broadmoor File No.1095, *supra,* n.19, gives Roderick's date and place of birth as February 10, 1854, 144a Oxford Street, and newspaper reports in 1874 gave his age as 18 and 19 and those of 1882 as 28. The 1861 census records a Charles M'lean, his son, also

built the Maclean Buildings in the Strand and that one of his brothers was married to the sister of Augustus Harris, the lessee of the Drury Lane Theatre. He claimed a brother living in Brighton and one in Australia. (It is unclear whether he had two or three brothers.) He had a sister living in Croydon, the Annie to whom the previously quoted letter had been written. It seems that it was this sister who, since the death of his father, had been supporting him with a monthly remittance from the rent of a house she owned in Croydon and that the crisis which led to the events in Windsor came about because she had not been able to let the house for the previous year and had written to Maclean telling him that she would be unable to send his remittance for March.

On February 16 Maclean had put down a deposit on a revolver with a local pawnbroker, giving his name as Campbell and saying that he was off to join the Cape Mounted Rifles. On February 22 he sold a woollen scarf and his concertina, which he used to play well into the night, paid the balance owing on the revolver to the pawnbroker, purchased some shot from a gunsmith,[67] and set off from Portsmouth saying he was going to London to seek help from Augustus Harris.[68] Two days later he had arrived in

---

Charles, and a 15 year-old nephew, Edward, as residents of 144a Oxford Street - but no Roderick. According to some reports, Charles Maclean lost a small fortune in a banking crash, which may have been that of Overend and Gurney.

67. The details of the purchase of the gun and shot were given at Maclean's committal proceedings and trial, *The Times* (London), Mar. 11, 1882, at 10, col. c. and Apr. 20, 1882, at 11, col. b.

68. *Sussex Daily News*, Mar. 4, 1882; *Sussex Daily News*, Mar. 9, 1882; *Evening News* (Portsmouth), Mar. 3, 1882; *The Times* (London), Mar. 4, 1882, at 10, col. b.

Windsor.[69]

69. Details provided on Maclean's admission to Broadmoor in order to establish his place of settlement show at least 30 different addresses in the 10 years up to 1883, mainly in London and the South of England but stretching from Sunderland to Boulogne and Margate to Weston-super-Mare, File No. 1095, *supra* n.19. Kensington eventually accepted liability as Maclean's parish of settlement, Rutherglen to Even Hare, PRO: HO 144/95/A14281, "Attempted Assassination of Her Majesty Queen Victoria by R. Maclean", f. 22.

In the immediate aftermath of the shooting, however, the signs of madness were not entirely clear. Almost immediately the Home Office and Scotland Yard received a letter from Charles E. Maw, a witness at Johann Most's trial, with an old copy of *Freiheit*, suggesting that Most might be behind the shooting.[70] Some papers reported that Maclean's forename was Patrick, that he was Irish and that he had spent time in a lunatic asylum in Dublin.[71] Among the items found on Maclean when he was searched was a paper on which was written

> "Reynold's Newspaper gives us as correct an idea of the wide difference that divides the people of England as any newspaper in the world. I venerate the free, outspoken principles of an unbiased thinker. Roderick Maclean, 27 February 1882, Windsor, Berks."[72]

Reynold's Newspaper was a radical publication, the first to voice concern about methods being used by the unit that was to become Special Branch,[73] but this news brought forth a

70. *Id.* at f. 1. A correspondent of John Brown, Victoria's personal attendant, suggested that Maclean might have been put up to the incident to create a run on the Stock Exchange, Letter from E. Keet Campbell to Brown, RA L14/125.
71. See Harcourt's statements to the House of Commons about Maclean's alleged Irish connections, 266 Parl. Deb., HC (3rd ser.) 2042 (1882) and 268 Parl. Deb., HC. (3rd ser.) 541 (1882); *Daily Telegraph* (London), Mar. 4, 1882, at 8, col. e.
72. *Sussex Daily News*, Mar. 4, 1882.
73. B. Porter, 1987, *supra* n. 39, 79 and 133-138.

leader from it dissociating itself from Maclean's action.[74] When being taken to Windsor Police Station after his arrest Maclean claimed that he had acted as he had from starvation and a letter found on him and signed "Roderick Maclean, March 2, Waiting Room, Great Western Railway" read

> "I should not have done this crime had you, as you should have done, paid the 10s per week instead of offering me the insulting sum of 6s per week, and expecting me to live on it. So you perceive the great good a little money would have done, had you not treated me as a fool, and set me more than ever against those bloated aristocrats, led by that old lady Mrs. Vic, who is an accursed[75] robber in all senses."[76]

At Portsmouth he was reported to have been a "voluble talker and a zealous politician of strong Radical views ... accustomed to denounce the treatment Mr Bradlaugh had experienced in the House of Commons".[77] Moreover,

---

74. *Reynold's Newspaper* (London), Mar. 5, 1882, at 5, col. c.
75. "An incensed robber" according to the *Windsor and Eton Gazette*, Mar. 4, 1882, and *Daily Telegraph* (London), Apr. 20, 1882, at 4, col. c.
76. *The Times* (London) Mar. 4, 1882, at 10, col. b. The letter was not addressed to anyone. Earlier in the afternoon Maclean had been ushered out of the first class waiting room at the railway station by the station master. Perhaps he was interrupted while writing the letter. It never emerged whom it was for.
77. *The Times* (London) Mar. 4, 1882, at 10, col. b. Lewis Harcourt wrote in his Journal for 2 March "... as if this [the news of Maclean's exploit] was not enough bad news for one day a special edition of the *Echo* has just now (10.40 pm) announced the election of Bradlaugh for Northampton", *Journal of Lewis Harcourt*, (Mar. 3, 1882), *supra* n. 18. Charles Bradlaugh was the republican M.P. for Northampton who was unable properly to take his seat

although by all accounts Maclean looked wretched when arrested, some found his plea of starvation difficult to reconcile with his possession of the revolver. Furthermore, his clever cross-examination of witnesses, when first brought before the magistrates, and his attempt to manipulate the legal process suggested something far removed from insanity. This, and many other perceived similarities to Guiteau, from the use of a revolver at a railway station[78] to Maclean's "repulsive appearance",[79] lead some papers to explain the assault by imitation - "Had there been no Guiteau ... there would have been no Maclean".[80]

---

in the House of Commons because the House refused to allow him, as a self-proclaimed atheist, either to affirm or to swear allegiance to the sovereign. On February 22, 1882 he was excluded for the third time in two years from the House and on March 2, 1882 was re-elected for the second. See W.L. Arnstein, *The Bradlaugh Case* (1965). It has been pointed out, *supra* n. 65, that some papers reported that Maclean's novel was entitled "The Fourth Oath." *The Daily News*, Mar. 4, 1882, at 5, col. b. while favouring "The Fourth Path" as the more likely title, commented that the other one sounded like a reference to Bradlaugh's career.

78. *Manchester Guardian*, as reported in *St. James's Gazette* (London), Mar. 3, 1882, at 12, col. b.
79. *Evening News* (Portsmouth), Mar. 3, 1882, at 2, col. a.
80. *Evening News* (Portsmouth), Mar. 4, 1882, at 2, col. a.

The Magistrates' Hearing

The place from which Maclean had discharged his revolver was some 13 yards from the spot where the Queen's carriage had drawn up for her and he had fired it as the carriage was moving towards him. (Accounts which would have Maclean's shot fired either before Victoria had alighted from the train or as she was doing so or as she was walking to her carriage[81] are clearly inaccurate.)[82] Before he could fire a second time[83] Maclean had been overpowered by a Superintendent Hayes, who seized him, James Burnside, a photographer,[84] who disarmed him, and two boys from Eton, one of whom, Gordon Chesney Wilson, belaboured him (and a bystander[85]) over the head with his umbrella. It was at first surmised from the "light" report made by the gun, the lack of any mark on the Queen's carriage, and the failure to find

---

81. *The Times* (London), Mar. 3, 1882, at 9, col. a; 2 J. Jeaffreson, *Victoria, Queen and Empress,* 183 (1893); G. Barnett Smith, *Life of Her Majesty Queen Victoria Compiled from all Available Sources,* 411 (1887); S. Weintraub, *Victoria, Biography of a Queen,* 450 (1987).

82. See RA Queen Victoria's Journal, (Mar. 2, 1882), reprinted in 3 Buckle, *supra* n. 16, at 265, the note from Ponsonby to Harcourt, (Mar. 2, 1882), quoted in 1 A. Gardner, *The Life of Sir William Harcourt,* 405 (1923), and the letter from the Queen to the Princess Royal, (Mar. 6, 1882), reprinted in *Beloved Mama: Private Correspondence of Queen Victoria and the German Crown Princess, 1878-1885,* 116 (R. Fulford ed. 1981).

83. Though evidence given at the remand hearing and later was that the revolver had been discharged twice, *The Times* (London), Mar. 4, 1882, at 10, col. a.

84. *The Illustrated London News,* Mar. 11, 1882, printed a photograph of Maclean and an illustration of the incident by Burnside. *The Graphic,* March 11, 1882, also printed a photograph and sketches.

85. A textbook example of "transferred" justification, see the evidence of William McCloskie as reported in *The Times* (London), Mar. 11, 1882, at 10, col. c, and the *Windsor and Eton Express,* Mar. 11, 1882.

any bullet, that Maclean had fired only a blank. But when Maclean's gun was examined, the revolver was found to contain two discharged cartridges, two loaded ones and two empty chambers, and Maclean himself was found to have 14 cartridges loaded with ball upon him.

The charge on which Hayes sought a remand on the evening of the incident was shooting at the Queen with intent to do her grievous bodily harm. The following morning, at about 9 o'clock, a bullett was found which, it was believed, had ricocheted off a railway truck standing on the other side of the Queen's carriage from Maclean and in line with both. The truck, however, was no longer in position, having been moved to Reading before the bullet was found. At 10 o'clock Maclean wrote out the following statement:

> "I am not guilty of the charge of shooting with the intention of causing actual bodily harm. My object was by frightening the Queen to alarm the public, with the result of having my grievances respected - viz, such as the pecuniary straits in which I have been situated. All the circumstances tend to prove this statement."

His statement went on to point out that if he really had wanted to injure the Queen he could have more certainly done so when she was on foot between railway and horse-drawn carriage, a point coincidentally made by a spectator whose letter about it to *The Times* was printed in the column alongside Maclean's admission.[86] Maclean's admission stated

---

86. Letter from R.C.P., *The Times* (London), Mar. 4, 1882, at 10, col. b.

that he had fired at the wheels of the carriage but the recoil of the gun could have pushed his arm upwards. He finished

> "If her Majesty will accept this explanation and allow the words 'with intent to intimidate her', instead of 'with intent to cause grievous bodily harm', to be inserted in that count, I will offer all assistance in my power to bring the charge herein specified to a speedy conclusion.
>
> I hope Her Majesty will accept the only consolation I can offer - namely, that I had no intention whatever of causing her any injury."

At the next remand hearing shortly afterwards, the charge had been raised to shooting at the Queen with intent to murder her. When cross-examining Hayes, who had given evidence that he had seen Maclean with the gun in his hand outstretched at shoulder height, Maclean had Hayes agree that he had not actually seen Maclean fire the gun and that it would be impossible for anyone to continue to hold the gun in the position in which he had seen Maclean holding it. Maclean similarly got other witnesses to admit that they had seen him only after the gun had been fired. Thus no prosecution witness was actually able to testify to Maclean's having aimed at the Queen. Under Maclean's cross-examination Hayes also admitted telling Maclean, before Maclean wrote his admission, that the charge would not be a capital one and that he had not cautioned Maclean that the admission would be used in evidence.

Some newspapers took this skilful conduct of his defence as a clear indication that Maclean was not only sane but cunning to boot.[87] An intent to intimidate without more would clearly take the case out of the category of treason and bring it within the 1842 Act.

Victoria was very concerned that none of her closest entourage who had seen the shooting, and particularly John Brown, be called to give evidence.[88] Fortunately for her, by the time of committal proceedings on March 10 witnesses had been found who would say that they had seen Maclean aim at the carriage. Furthermore, the truck from which it was believed the bullet had ricocheted had been located. It turned out to have been covered with a tarpaulin with painted figures on it. The top of one of these figures (a seven, not a four as Maclean might have feared) was marked and a railway inspector testified that the site of the mark would have been 5 feet 5 inches above the ground. He also testified that when he had found the bullet it had had a spot of paint on it which he had washed off.[89] At the previous remand hearing another railway inspector, in whose company he had been at the time, had also testified to washing the end of the bullet, though he was not reported as having mentioned any paint.[90] Maclean was still not represented at these proceedings, though his family was. He is not reported as having questioned any of the witnesses and he reserved his defence. He was committed for trial for high treason, the punishment for which was drawing followed by a public

---

87. Eg. *County Chronicle* (Reading), Mar. 11, 1882.
88. RA *Queen Victoria's Journal*, (Mar. 5 & 10, 1882); Letters from the Queen, (Mar. 2 & undated, 1882), RA L14/106 and 115.
89. Charles Noble, *The Times* (London), Mar. 11, 1882, at 10, col. a.
90. Joseph Turner, *The Times* (London), Mar. 4, 1882, at 10, col. a.

hanging, though the Queen could commute it to a public decapitation followed by quartering of the body.[91]

91. Treason, Act 1814, 54 Geo. 3, ch. 146, ss 1 and 2; Forfeiture Act, 1871, 33 and 34 Vict., ch. 23, s. 31. Since the Capital Punishment Amendment Act, 1868, 31 and 32 Vict., ch. 24, the executions of murderers had taken place in prisons but the Act applied only to murder. The last persons sentenced to be hung, decapitated and quartered were the Fenian insurrectionists of 1867 but they were reprieved and would not have been quartered if they had not been, see 187 Parl. Deb., HC (3rd. ser.) 89 and 1131, HJL (3rd. ser.) 1098 (1867), and R. Kee, *The Green Flag: A History of Irish Nationalism*, 330-347 (1972). The last persons actually beheaded in England for treason were the Cato Street conspirators in 1820, see J. Stanhope, *The Cato Street Conspiracy* (1962). Later the same year there were decapitations for treason in Scotland, P. Ellis and s. Mac A'Ghobhainn, *The Scottish Insurrection of 1820*, 270-280 (1970). See also "Executing Traitors" in V. Gattrell, *The Hanging Tree: Execution and the English People*, 298-321 (1994).

The Choice Before the Government

The dilemma facing the Government was the familiar one in cases of this kind: either to treat it as a relatively minor incident in an attempt to allay public alarm and reduce the amount and type of publicity it would attract, or to treat it as a very serious attempt on the monarch and risk the opposite effect. The first decision that the Government's approach was to affect was that of whether to have both Houses of Parliament present an Address to the Queen congratulating her on her escape. This had last been done in May 1842 after John Francis had discharged a pistol at the Queen in Hyde Park.[92] When news of Maclean's arrest broke, individuals, organisations and foreign governments fell over themselves in a rush to send telegraphs and deliver messages and addresses of loyalty, thanks and congratulations[93] and

92. 63 Parl. Deb., HL (3rd. ser.) 995 and HC (3rd. ser.) 1014 (1842).

93. PRO: HO 45/9619A/14281B and 14281C contain the addresses sent by various organisations, and discussions of the finer points of protocol connected with submitting an Address, such as who had the right to present one in person, and with responding to it. The most interesting of these points related to the Address from "The Bishops of the Roman Catholic Church in England". The draft reply used that appellation and addressed Cardinal Manning as "Your Eminence". The appellation was held to be objectionable and was altered to "The Roman Catholic Bishops in England". Manning's designation was also altered since it was improper for the Queen responding "through the Secretary of State to a body of her subjects, ... without previous consent given, [to] recognise and answer one of them by a title which has not been conferred or sanctioned by her". There are echoes here of the defence of Anglican ecclesiastical titles mounted by the Ecclesiastical Titles Assumption Act, which had been passed in 1851 and replaced 20 years later. In January 1870, while attending the Vatican Council which later in the year declared the Pope to be infallible, Manning had become the first person to be (unsuccessfully) summonsed under the Act. On this and Manning's being accorded strictly unwarranted titles and precedence shortly after 1882, see *Cobbett v.*

Victoria was keen that Parliament should join in too.[94] This was the occasion when she remarked "It is worth being shot at - to see how much one is loved".[95] Gladstone's first thought, however, was against an Address from Parliament:[96]

> "... the dominant feeling in my mind has been that the whole of these deplorable attempts on the life of the Queen have proceeded from men of weak and morbid minds; that to such minds notoriety is the very highest reward and inducement that can be offered, and that from their point of view an Address, which puts the Houses of Parliament in motion under their impulsion, is of itself in the nature of such reward and inducement. Finally that the best means of dealing with these cases are to keep from them what feeds the vain imagination and to administer

---

Archbishop Manning, The Times (London), Jan. 31, 1870, at 11, col. e, 204 Parl. Deb., HC (3rd ser.) 1264 and 1359 (1871), O. Chadwick, *The Victorian Church Part 1,* 275-306 (1966), E. Norman, *Anti-Catholicism in Victorian England,* 52-79 (1968), Rawls, "The Papal Aggression of 1850: A Study in Victorian Anti-Catholicism" in G. Parsons (Ed.), *Religion in Victorian Britain, Vol 4: Interpretations,* 115-134 (1988), and L. Strachey, *Eminent Victorians,* 57 and 96 (1986).

94. Letter from Ponsonby to Granville, (Mar. 3, 1882), and from the Queen to Granville, Mar. 5, 1882, Granville Papers, PRO 30/29/31 and 30/29/40 both referred to in 1 *The Political Correspondence of Mr Gladstone and Lord Granville* 1876-1882, 347 (A. Ramm ed. 1962); Letter from the Queen to Gladstone, (Mar. 5, 1882), reprinted in 2 Guedalla, *supra* n. 17, at 181[841].

95. Letter from the Queen to the Princess Royal, (Mar. 6, 1882), reprinted in Fulford *supra* n. 82, at 116. Victoria counted 138 telegrams on the day immediately following the shooting and 68 on the day after that.

96. Letter from Gladstone to Granville (Mar. 3, 1882), reprinted in Ramm, *supra,* n. 94, at 347; Letter from Gladstone to Northcote (Mar. 3, 1882), reprinted in Matthew, *supra,* n. 37, at 217.

sharp judicial sentences ..."[97]

However, by the time the Cabinet met on Saturday afternoon it had been established that Maclean had used live ammunition and, in the light of this and Tory stirrings, the Cabinet agreed there should be an Address.[98]Moreover, with foreign governments sending Addresses to Victoria, the absence of one from her own might have appeared a calculated snub. Gladstone went along with the decision reluctantly but admitted to the Queen that he had perhaps accorded "too much weight to the length of time during which no Address had been presented".[99]The address was moved on 6 March[100] and duly presented to her at Windsor by a Parliamentary delegation on the following Friday.[101]

The more important decision that had to be made concerned the trial. What should the charge be and should

97. Letter from Gladstone to Ponsonby, (Mar. 3, 1882), part of which is reprinted in 2 Guedalla, *supra* n. 17. at 180[839]; Letter from Gladstone to Ponsonby, (Mar. 3, 1882), RA L14/108; Ballman, *supra* n. 37, 231-237.

98. Note 4 of Cabinet Meeting and Letter from Gladstone to Northcote, (Mar. 4, 1882), reprinted in Matthew, *supra* n. 37, at 218.

99. Letter from Gladstone to the Queen, (Mar. 4, 1882), RA A55/36, the first part of which is reprinted in 2 Guedalla, *supra* n. 17, at 180[840].

100. For the Parliamentary proceedings see 267 Parl. Deb., HL (3rd ser.), 163 (1882) and 267 Parl. Deb., HC (3rd ser.), 223 (1882).

101. In Hughenden Church, where Victoria had placed a tablet in memory of Disraeli, who had died the year before, is a stained glass window commemorating Victoria's escape from Maclean, Longford, *supra* n. 32a, 548 and S. Lee, *Queen Victoria: A Biography*, 470 (1904). It is in the north west corner of the church, depicts St George and St David, and was placed there by the then tenant of Hughenden Manor, Sir Samuel "Bullocky Sam" Wilson, the father of one of the Eton schoolboys who had attacked Maclean.

a special commission be issued to try it?[102] Since the passage of the Treason Acts of 1800 and 1842, the procedures for the trial of traitors and murderers had been the same where the treason alleged consisted of an overt act of killing, endangering the life of, or causing bodily harm to, or wounding, the monarch, or of an attempt to do any of these things. Since 1842, however, it had been possible to proceed against those who had not actually posed a threat to the monarch's life by means of a lesser offence and this had been used against Bean in 1842 and against the only two other persons who had attempted to discharge firearms near the Queen since 1842, William Hamilton in 1849,[103] and Arthur O' Connor in 1872. In these cases, however, there had been no live ammunition. Moreover, Victoria was still galled by the light sentence imposed on O'Connor. Hamilton and Pate, who had also been convicted under the 1842 Act after hitting Victoria with a cane in Piccadilly in 1850,[104] had been sentenced to the maximum punishment allowed by the Act, seven years' transportation, although their assaults had been far from the most serious that could be covered by the Act while falling short of treason. But Baron Cleasby had sentenced O'Connor to only one year's imprisonment with

102. For a contemporary review of the state of the law of treason prompted by the Maclean trial, see Harrison, "Curiosities of the Law of Treason and History of the Law of Treason", 31 *Fortnightly Review*, 587 & 698 (1882); and for a justification (from a republican organ) of laws giving special protection to the person of the sovereign in a constitutional monarchy, see "The Morality of Laws Against Regicide" in *The Spectator* (London), Mar. 11, 1882, 324.

103. *R. v. Hamilton*, 7 St. Tr. N.S. 1130 (1848-50).

104. *R. v. Pate*, 8 St. Tr. N.S. 2. (1850-58).

hard labour and a 20 stroke whipping. Victoria had felt threatened by the prospect of O'Connor's early release and had suggested that those who attacked or alarmed her should be exiled.[105] Transportation was no longer available, and after some haggling O'Connor had agreed to go into voluntary exile in Australia in return for having the remainder of his sentence and the whipping respited.[106] But there had been no power to keep him in Australia[107] and at the beginning of 1874 he had returned to London. On 5 May the following year, as Victoria was holding a Drawing Room, O'Connor had been arrested at the very spot where he had previously brandished a gun at her. On this occasion he was committed to Hanwell Lunatic Asylum where he still was in March 1882.[108] Gladstone had been Prime Minister in 1872, had agreed with the Queen's sentiments then, and now was concerned to prevent a repetition.[109]

---

105. Letter from the Queen to Gladstone, (Apr.11, 1872), reprinted in 1 P. Guedalla, *The Queen and Mr Gladstone, 1845-1879*, 344[452] (1933); Letter from the Queen to Princess Louise, (Apr.13, 1872), reprinted in *Darling Child: Private Correspondence of Queen Victoria and the Crown Princess of Prussia, 1871-1878* 38 (R. Fulford ed. 1976).
106. Letters from Gladstone to the Queen, (Apr. 11-12, 1872 and Dec. 3, 1872), reprinted in 1 Guedalla, *supra* n. 105, at 345[454] and 387 [503].
107. A conditional release under s.5 of the Criminal Lunatics Act, 1867, 30 Vict., ch. 12, which would have permitted O'Connor's rearrest on his return, was not available since O'Connor was not a criminal lunatic.
108. PRO: HO 144/10963; "The Boy O'Connor at Buckingham Palace", *The Times* (London), May . 14, 1875, at 5, col. c, reprinting an item from the *British Medical Journal,* I, 658 (May 15, 1875) and "The Boy O'Connor", *The Times* (London), Mar. 15, 1875, at 7, col. 7e (reprinting one from the *Pall Mall Gazette*).
109. Letter from Gladstone to Ponsonby, (Mar. 2, 1882), reprinted in 2 Guedalla, *supra* n. 17, at 179 [836]; RA *Queen Victoria's Journal*, (Mar. 8, 1882).

By 10 March the course which the trial was to take had been determined. Howard Vincent, the Head of the CID, to whom Maw's letter about Freiheit had been referred, had reported two days later that the shooting

> "was the work of a lunatic, whose antecedents have been fully ascertained, and in no shape or form traceable to any English or Foreign Political Society."[110]

This did not come as a complete surprise to many, if the press is to be believed, so beloved, admired and respected was Victoria.

> "It is a tradition in England that only a madman can dream of conspiring against the life of the Queen"

was a view from abroad.[111] If expected, it nevertheless came as a relief to most. *The Spectator* commented:

> "It is a subject for gratitude to Providence that the Queen was not killed, and an even greater one that the intending assassin was not an Irishman. He might very well have been a Macarthy, instead of a Maclean, and still have been

---

110. Vincent's report, (Mar. 4, 1882), PRO: HO 144/95/A14281, *supra* n. 69, at f.2.

111. *Le Telegraphe* (Paris) as reported in *The Daily Telegraph* (London), Mar. 4, 1882, at 5, col. h. See, for example, Alderson B. sentencing Pate: "I would fain believe it is the privilege and boast of the country that no man but a madman would attack the most gracious Sovereign of this country. I believe it is as great a proof of insanity as it is possible for a person to give", *R. v. Pate*, *supra* n. 104.

only a murderer; but no conceivable evidence would have convinced the country that the Land Leaguers were not responsible, or have induced them for half-a-century to come to trust any popular party in Ireland."[112]

On 7 March Harcourt had told Ponsonby that the charge would be treason with intent to murder and with intent to do grievous bodily harm (under the Treason Act 1795).[113] On the day before Gladstone accompanied the Parliamentary delegation to deliver the Address, he wrote to inform Victoria of the results of the deliberations of the Home Secretary and Law Officers.

"Your Majesty's Law Officers are sensible how important it is that there should in this case be a power of imprisonment without any limit of time.

The indictment will be for intent to murder, but this intent is, in the case of Your Majesty's person, of itself treason: so that the capital offence could be commuted, upon a verdict of Guilty, into imprisonment for life.

It is thought by far the most probable ... that the friends of Maclean will defend him on the ground of insanity. And the Law Officers seem at present nor inclined to resist that plea à l'outrance. For, if it be admitted, the man may be imprisoned without limit of time; whereas, if it were overthrown, the parties might be driven to another line

112. *The Spectator* (London), Mar. 4, 1882, 284, col. b.

113. Letter from Harcourt to Ponsonby, (Mar. 7, 1882), RA L14/112. The joinder was made possible by Treason Act, 1842, 5 and 6 Vict., ch. 51, s. 1, see the Law Officers' Memorandum, (July 8, 1842), RA M667/71.

of defence, and might try to show that the intent was only to alarm. For, if by any chance the jury were to accept this plea, the term of imprisonment would be limited and comparatively short.

The depositions not being yet complete the Law Officers do not give a final opinion; but they appear to have little doubt of obtaining in the one shape or the other, the power of imprisonment for life."[114]

Or, as Victoria summarised the strategy in her Journal, Maclean would be proceeded against for High Treason but

"If there should be any fear of his not being convicted for intent to murder, the plea of insanity will be brought forward; this might be accepted in order to ensure his incarceration for life."[115]

Victoria had been due to go abroad for a few weeks and, just as she departed for Menton, Gladstone was able to tell her that a special commission to try Maclean would be issued to Lord Coleridge, the Lord Chief Justice, and one other judge - in the event Baron Huddleston.[116] *The Law Journal* doubted the wisdom of "giving so dignified an aspect to Maclean's act" and pointed out that one result of his being tried by special commission was that there could be no

114. Letter from Gladstone to the Queen, (Mar. 9, 1882), RA L14/116.
115. RA *Queen Victoria's Journal*, (Mar. 10, 1882).
116. Letter from Gladstone to the Queen, (Mar. 13-14, 1882), RA L14/122.

appeal to the court for Crown Cases Reserved.[117]

117 It also remarked that since Maclean was charged with treason the trial could not be removed under Palmer's Act to the Central Criminal Court, where any and all the judges could sit, and where all previous assaults on the Queen had been tried, though the Attorney-General could have removed the case to the Queen's Bench, "*Obiter Dicta*", 17 *Law Journal* 133 and 185 (1882).

Preparations for the Trial

When Maclean was questioned after first being taken into custody, he had been examined by a Dr William Holderness who was reported to have pronounced him sane.[118] Some papers reported that another doctor, named by at least one as the Queen's physician,[119] had examined him too and formed the same opinion.[120] He was also interviewed by a solicitor acting for his family. To allay any fear that Maclean's act was politically motivated and to counter the impression that Maclean was sane, the solicitor wrote a letter to *The Times* in which he said that a doctor who had been reported as having found Maclean sane had told the solicitor that he had been misreported.[121] This drew a response from Holderness which confirmed the meeting with the solicitor but denied that he had in any way indicated his opinion of Maclean's sanity.[122] Holderness's letter in turn prompted one from Oliver Maurice, the doctor at Reading Prison to which Maclean had been transferred on the evening of 4 March, who had examined him almost daily since then. It expressed amusement at Holderness's claim that he had been assured by "the Superintendent of Police that no other medical man than myself has examined the prisoner" and pointed out that, apart from Maurice himself, Manning had also examined

---

118. *Windsor and Eton Express*, Mar. 4, 1882; *The Times* (London), Mar. 3, 1882, at 5, col.e.
119. *Sussex Daily News*, Mar. 3, 1882.
120. For example, *Evening News* (Portsmouth), Mar. 3, 1882, at 2, col. a.
121. Letter from "The Solicitor to the Family", (Mar. 3, 1882), *The Times* (London), Mar. 6, 1882, at 6, col. b.
122. Letter "The Shooting at the Queen", (Mar. 6, 1882), *The Times* (London) Mar. 13, 1882, at 9, col. f.

Maclean at the request of his family.[123] But Maurice failed to note that the point of Holderness's claim was that he had been the only one to have examined Maclean when the family solicitor had written his letter. Maurice's letter was disingenuous in another way. He said he had been asked by the Treasury Solicitor, Augustus Stephenson, to report on Maclean. This was indeed true, but, in fact, Maurice had questioned Stephenson's authority to ask him for such a report, and suggested that the application for one should be made through the Prison Commissioners.[124] Maurice was rebuked for discussing the case in the press but it was not only in obtaining a medical report that Stephenson met with a request that he proceed through the Prison Commissioners: his application to the Governor of Reading Prison for a copy of Maclean's warrant of commitment did so too.[125]

Stephenson encountered other frustrations in the preparation of the case. Instructed by the Attorney-General to obtain an independent medical report on Maclean, Stephenson instructed Dr Edgar Sheppard to produce one. But Stephenson did so without first submitting Sheppard's name to the Home Secretary, as Harcourt understood he had been instructed to do. When Harcourt learned what had been done he was angered on three counts: firstly, because he had

---

123. Letter "The Prisoner Maclean", (Mar. 13, 1882), *The Times* (London) Mar. 16, 1882, at 10, col. b. Manning first examined Maclean on the 6 March and was to do so again on 30 March.

124. Letters from Stephenson to Maurice, (Mar. 11, 1882), and from Maurice to Stephenson, (Mar. 13, 1882), PRO; HO 144/95/A14281, *supra* n. 69, at f. 5. The Commissioners had been established only since 1877.

125. Letters from Stephenson to Liddell, (Mar. 16, 1882), and from Blyth to Stephenson, (Mar. 15, 1882), PRO: HO 144/95/A14281, *supra* n. 69, at f. 57.

not been consulted, secondly because he had never heard of Sheppard, and thirdly because he had now learned that Sheppard had been involved in O'Connor's trial. In this latter respect Harcourt was completely wrong, as Adolphus Liddell, Under Secretary of State at the Home Office, quickly told him.[126] Sheppard had been one of the doctors employed by the Government to produce a pre-trial report on O'Connor but he had reported him completely sane and had taken no part in the trial.[127] However, by this time, Sheppard had carried out his examination. There was not really any question of countermanding his instructions, as Stephenson offered to do. Instead all the papers in the case, including Sheppard's report, were sent to Dr William Orange, the Medical Superintendent at Broadmoor, whom Harcourt

---

126. Letter from Liddell to Harcourt, (Mar. 25, 1882), MS. Harcourt dep. 96, fol. 65.

127. The defence had been handicapped in the O'Connor case in that it had had several medical witnesses, including Harrison Tuke, prepared to testify to O'Connor's insanity, but O'Connor himself would have none of it and, to everyone's surprise, pleaded guilty. Consequently the defence had to introduce the evidence in support of a motion to arrest judgment on the ground that O'Connor had been unfit to plead, *The Times* (London), Apr. 10, 11 and 12, 1872, at 11, col. c, 11, col. c, and 11, col. a; *Annual Register Remarkable Trials* 209 (1871). Sheppard's critical comments on Tuke's behaviour and Tuke's reply can be found in the articles entitled "The Case of Arthur O'Connor", *The Lancet*, I, 535 and 571 (Apr. 20 and 27, 1872). The controversy resurfaced when O'Connor was rearrested in 1875, see the articles by Tuke, Sheppard, Crighton Browne and Sabben, *British Medical Journal* I, 672, 685, 729, 756, and 757 (May 22 and 29, and June 6, 1875). Controversies such as this, with doctors criticising each other's forensic conduct in print, were not unusual, see, for example, those following the trials of Townley and Buranelli, R. Smith, *Trial by Medicine: Insanity and Responsibility in Victorian Trials*, 124-142 (1981).

insisted was the person he always used in such cases.[128] Lewis Harcourt may have slightly misunderstood matters when he recorded in his journal for 31 March

> "As to Maclean there is no doubt of his insanity and so anxious is the H.S. to have it proved that he has given orders for Dr Sheppard to be instructed by the Solicitor to the Treasury Solicitor to go down to Reading Gaol to examine him."[129]

On 4 April J. Haynes, the solicitor who had been instructed by Maclean's family to organise his defence, wrote to the Home Office saying that the sole defence would be one of insanity. Haynes was concerned at the expense of calling all the witnesses who could testify to Maclean's state of mind at various times in his life. Haynes had heard that Sheppard had examined Maclean and thought that, if Sheppard's conclusion were the same as that of Manning, their evidence would be sufficient to establish Maclean's insanity at the time of the offence, and the expense of calling Drs Maudsley, Goodrich, and Sheldon (from Wells) would be spared. To this end Haynes offered Stephenson a sight of all the defence papers in the case in return for one of Sheppard's report.[130] Stephenson, who had already seen Manning's report, rejected

128. Letters from Stephenson to Liddell, (Mar. 22, 1882), from Harcourt to Liddell, (Mar. 24, 1882), from Stephenson to Liddell, (Mar. 25, 1882), Minute by Liddell, (Mar. 3, 1882) and Letter from Stephenson to Black, (Mar. 3, 1882), PRO: HO 144/95/A14281, *supra* n. 69, at ff. 8, 25, 10 and 11.

129. *Journal of Lewis Harcourt*, (Mar. 3, 1882), *supra* n. 18, at f. 104.

130. Letter from Haynes to Home Office, (Apr. 4, 1882), PRO: HO 144/95/A14281, *supra* n. 69, at f. 15.

the offer, commenting that "the Crown must hold aloof from the defence and that the burden of proving the alleged insanity of the Prisoner must rest with his advisers".[131] In the face of this rejection Montague Williams, who had been instructed for the defence,[132] advised calling at least Maudsley and Hitchins, and Haynes then applied to the Treasury for money to pay for their attendance at the trial.[133] Harcourt and James, the Attorney-General, agreed that Hitchins's and Sheldon's attendances should be paid for, but not Maudsley's.[134] In the event, as has been seen, the defence called all these witnesses and more.

In opening the case for the prosecution at the trial the Attorney-General repeated that a defence of insanity "was the prisoner's business to substantiate, and it must, therefore, be left entirely to the learned counsel who represented the accused" but he gave no hint that this was likely to prove difficult. Indeed he did all he could to assist the defence without actually agreeing that Maclean was insane. He

---

131. Letter from Stephenson to Haynes, (Apr. 5, 1882), PRO: HO 144/95/A14281, *supra* n. 69, at f.15.

132. Williams was one of the leading criminal advocates of his day. His reminiscences of the trial, however, are singularly uninformative. The only information they reveal that is not apparent from other sources is Williams's belief that it was Victoria's wish that Maclean be legally represented. According to *The Englishman* (London), Apr. 1, 1882, at 356, the Treasury paid his fees, but, if they did, Williams was not aware of it, see M. Williams, *Later Leaves: Being the Further Reminiscences of Montague Williams, QC*, 182-193 (1891).

133. Letters from Haynes to Stephenson, (Apr. 14, 1882), from Stephenson to Haynes, (Apr. 15, 1882), from Haynes to Secretary to Lords of the Treasury, (Apr. 17, 1882), PRO: HO 144/95/A14281, *supra* n.69, at f.15.

134. Minute by Harcourt, (Apr. 17, 1882), PRO: HO 144/95/A14281, *supra* n. 69, at f. 15.

explained that

> "At the time of the apprehension of the prisoner circumstances arose which made it advisable to inquire into his condition when he committed the offence ... and, no doubt, facts existed in relation to the condition of the prisoner's mind which would require very grave and patient consideration. There was, of course, no desire on the part of the prosecution to keep back any facts, for such a desire would be contrary to humanity and even opposed to justice. He would conclude by saying that if the prisoner should be held to be so insane as to be entitled to an acquittal, satisfaction would be felt by every subject of the Queen at the thought that it was not from the ranks of those who were sane that a hand had been raised against our gracious sovereign."

At the end of the case for the prosecution James offered Sheppard, Orange, and Maurice for cross-examination by the defence. In his closing speech he repeated that the prosecution agreed that Maclean's mind "was not in a healthy state" but that it was for the jury to determine whether he was insane. James finished by reminding the jury that if they acquitted Maclean on grounds of insanity he would not be set free but detained.

In summing up Lord Coleridge reminded the jury verbatim of the M'Naughten Rules without apparently indicating which of the medical witnesses' testimony was strictly congruent with them and which was not,[135] encouraged them towards a finding that Maclean was insane, "a merciful verdict [which] ... would save a man's life and ... protect society against a repetition of an outrage which had endangered a life most inestimably precious", but enjoined them to ensure that if they were to acquit Maclean they should make it expressly clear that they did so on the ground of insanity, else there might be no power to detain him. As Attorney-General, Coleridge had been involved in the O'Connor affair in 1872, both during O'Connor's trial, when he had led the prosecution and conducted a severe and controversial cross-examination of Tuke, and after. The jury required little time to consider their verdict and duly acquitted Maclean.[136]

---

135. For example Manning testified that Maclean would have been aware of the nature of his act and that it was wrong but that he had acted under an irresistible delusional impulse, Sheppard that he would have had no idea of right and wrong and have been unable to control his actions, and Orange that he would have known neither the nature of his act nor that it was wrong.

136. *The Times* (London) Apr. 20, 1882, at 11, cols. a-e.

Maclean in Broadmoor

The defence had contested none of the prosecution evidence, thus in effect admitting that Maclean intended to do Victoria at least grievous bodily harm. But Maclean was committed to Broadmoor maintaining that he never intended the Queen any harm and had not intended to shoot at her. He made this claim in an autobiography, *The History of My Life*, which he composed while on remand.[137] He repeated it in a letter to his sister,[138] in some of the unsuccessful petitions for release he submitted from Broadmoor,[139] and in an undated letter apparently prepared for public release, in which he added the argument that as the Queen could not be seen from where he was standing he can hardly have intended to shoot at her.[140]

---

137. *The Times* (London), Apr. 20, 1882, at 11, col. e. I have not found a copy of this autobiography. In the file on Maclean in Broadmoor, File No. 1095, *supra* n. 19 is a letter, or the draft or copy of a letter, dated 5 August 1894, from Maclean to Thomas Power O'Connor at the Sun Office in Tudor Street. The letter acknowledges O'Connor's criticisms "so kindly made" of some verse of Maclean and offers O'Connor, "'The History of My Life' which I think you will be interested to read as it is the record of a chequered career including besides minor affairs an escapade in Windsor in the year 1882. Expecting a reply under the initials R.E.M. in your Post Bag Column". O'Connor had founded the *Sunday Sun* in 1891 and changed its name to the *Weekly Sun* in 1893. In 1893 he also founded *The Sun*, an evening paper. The *Weekly Sun* had a large Post Bag column, *The Sun* had none. I have found no reply under the initials R.E.M. in the *Weekly Sun* from the start of August to the end of September 1894, nor any trace of the autobiography in *The Sun* or *Weekly Sun* for that period. The largest extracts from the autobiography I have found are in Reynolds's Newspaper (London), Apr. 23, 1882, 1d.
138. Letter from Maclean to Annie Maclean, (Mar. 9, 1883), File No. 1095, *supra* n. 19.
139. Petition, (Mar. undated, 1886), File No. 1095, *supra* n. 19.
140. File No. 1095, *supra* n. 19.

The public was reminded of Maclean's case in a curious way in 1895 and 1900. By 1892 James Burnside, the photographer who had disarmed him, had fallen on hard times. He wrote to the Home Secretary, pointing out that he had never received any public acknowledgment of his bravery, and asking if any government business could be put his way. This was the first of a series of fruitless letters, which became increasingly dotty after Burnside's part was taken over by his father. The main difficulty for Burnside was that Sir Henry Ponsonby was adamant that exactly who had been responsible for disabling Maclean had never been properly established at the time. Burnside Snr suspected that Superintendent Hayes, the policeman involved, had used his position to advance his own claim and disparage that of others,[141] even to the extent of bringing improper influence on Roger Errington, who was the main, and favourable, independent witness to Burnside Jnr's actions. The upshot was that in a final attempt to get satisfaction Burnside Snr threatened to reveal the Government's ingratitude by broadcasting it to the world, which he did - in the *Guernsey Times*.[142] In 1900 Burnside Snr took to print again to refute the claim made in *Mainly about People* that Major Gordon Wilson, the former umbrella wielding Eton schoolboy who was now holed up in Mafeking with Baden-Powell, had saved Victoria

---

141. "Police Superintendent Hayes loudly asserted that he was the man. And I was friendly with Hayes who had been my sergeant-major. But he never proved his case", Letter from Ponsonby to West, (Aug. 28, 1893), PRO: HO 144/V19056, "Claim by James Burnside for Recognition of his Son's Part in Disarming an Assassin of Queen Victoria, 1892-1900".

142. *The Guernsey Times*, June 29, July 6, 13, 20 & 27, and Aug. 3, 1895.

from Maclean.[143]

As for Maclean, the documentary evidence of the remainder of his life consists a serious of unsuccessful petitions for release, on one occasion to go to live on Mull, "the isle of his ancestors", and on another Australia,[144] several letters stretching over the years 1887 to 1899 which consist of threats to kill a cousin, whom Maclean considered to be associated with female voices that were tormenting him, two letters in 1894 and 1895 connected with his attempt to have some verses published, an unsuccessful attempt to initiate a correspondence with the Queen, and around 1917 some letters about his declining health and the sexual hallucinations he was having. He died in Broadmoor on 11 June 1921, according to the verdict of the jury at his inquest, from apoplexy.

---

143. "The Boy Who Saved the Queen", MAP (London), Mar. 17, 1900. Burnside despatched letters refuting the claim to several papers. One was used by the *Newcastle Daily Journal*, Mar. 20, 1900. The editor of *The Times* declined to publish Burnside's letter, it being "against his practice to contradict erroneous statements made in other journals." For the whole saga see PRO: HO 144/V19056, *supra* n. 141.

144. In File No. 1095, *supra* n. 19, and PRO: HO 144/95/A14281, *supra* n. 69, are petitions dated Feb. 18, 1884, May 18, 1885, Dec. 4, 1885, Mar. undated, 1886, Jan. 1, 1887, Oct. 10, 1887 and Apr. 3, 1905.

The Trial of Lunatics Act

On the second Sunday after the incident at Windsor the Rev. Coker Adams had treated his parishioners to a sermon on 2 *Samuel*, 1, 14: "How wast thou not afraid to stretch forth thine hand to destroy the Lord's anointed?". After the trial he published it. It took very great exception to the way Maclean and his predecessors had been treated and argued for the execution of traitors irrespective of their mental condition.[145] This view, however, was little echoed in the press whose general opinion was that Maclean was indubitably insane - "from the soles of his feet to the crown of his head"[146] - and his acquittal quite proper.[147] Though some concern was expressed at Maclean's having been at large in the first place and at the failure of the doctors at the trial to agree on the type of insanity from which Maclean suffered,[148] the conduct of the trial was compared very favourably with that of Guiteau in America, which had been turned into an arena in

---

145. C. Adams, *Protect the Queen: A Sermon Preached at Saham Toney, Norfolk, March 12, 1882.*

146. "The Maclean Case", *Medical Times and Gazette*, I, 443 (Apr. 29, 1882).

147. The press was as pleased with the Government's acceptance that Maclean was insane as with its rejection of pleas, mainly from America, for commuting the death sentence on the poisoner Lamson on grounds of his alleged insanity. Lamson had been convicted on March 14. The sentence was twice respited but Lamson was eventually executed on April 28, see "Correspondence with the United States Government Respecting the Postponement of Execution of the Sentence Passed upon the Convict Lamson", C. 3195, (HC Papers, 1882, v. 30, at p.1); "The Lamson Case", *British Medical Journal*, i, 584 (Apr. 22, 1882); *The Lancet*, i, 695 (Apr. 29, 1882); "The Last of Lamson", *Medical Times and Gazette*, i, 442 (Apr. 29, 1882); "Case of Lamson", 28 *Journal of Mental Science* 243 (1882); 2 M. Williams, *Leaves of a Life: Being the Reminiscences of Montague Williams, QC*, 182-193 (1890).

148. "The Maclean Case", *Medical Times and Gazette*, i, 444 (Apr. 29, 1882).

which rival schools and occupational groups within the psychiatric profession had battled for the law's imprimatur.[149] Such criticism as there was tended to be of the decision to dignify Maclean's offence by trying him for treason, especially as this precluded the possibility of his being whipped, as would have been possible had he been convicted of an offence under the 1842 Act.

As is well known, however, Victoria's sentiments were much more akin to those of Rev. Adams: she was almost as displeased by the outcome of the trial as she had been by that of O'Connor's, though it can hardly have come as a surprise to her. She had, after all, made an accurate summary of its future course in her Journal without giving any indication that it would displease her. She had returned from France just five days before the trial. "It really is too bad", she recorded in her Journal when she learned of the verdict.[150] But it is not entirely clear at exactly what she was aggrieved or what she had hoped would be done to Maclean. She was angry that the prosecution had made no attempt to cross-examine the defence witnesses, angry that Coleridge had referred the jury to the M'Naughten Rules,[151] and angry that

149. *Evening News* (Portsmouth), Mar. 4, 1882, at 2, col. a; 26 *Solicitors' Journal* 379 (Apr. 22, 1882); Rosenberg, *supra* n. 41.

150. RA *Queen Victoria's Journal*, (Apr. 19, 1882).

151. In his articles on the Maclean case Nigel Walker has defended Victoria against claims that she did not understand the law, but her criticism of Coleridge for referring to the M'Naughten Rules rather tells against him. The Rules were not responsible for the verdict in M'Naughten's case but were formulated after it. Had they been applied in the case M'Naughten would have been convicted and her protest to Peel at M'Naughten's acquittal was fair at the time, as Walker 1968, *supra* n. 44, at 188, states. The correct understanding of the position in 1882 is displayed in the Letter from

Maclean was to receive no more punishment than being locked up for life:

> "The bullet found - and *yet* he is only to be shut up. It is Oxford's case over again and Oxford himself said - when the other attempts followed - that if they had hung him these others would not have taken place ... And this always happens when a Liberal Government is in!"[152]

Above all Victoria was angry that Gladstone, Harcourt and James had intended the denouement of the affair all along. On the day after the acquittal Harcourt went down to Windsor to introduce the Corporation of London, who were to present an address of congratulation to Victoria on her escape from the gunman. Lewis Harcourt recorded in his Journal that

> "She was angry at the result of the Maclean trial as she does not understand the verdict of 'Not Guilty' and said to Sir Henry Ponsonby 'I know that Sir William Harcourt and Sir Henry James were determined to make him out mad all along'. She also said that she would not have an audience with him as she was much too excited."[153]

She must have been particularly disappointed about

Ponsonby to Gladstone, (Apr. 23, 1882), RA L14/141, which Walker reprints at p.189, but how much of this is Ponsonby and how much Victoria is difficult to say.

152. Letters from the Queen to Ponsonby, (Apr. 19, 1882), RA L14/133 and 134; 1 Bahlman, *supra* n. 37 at 254.

153. *Journal of Lewis Harcourt*, (Apr. 20, 1882), *supra* n. 18, at f. 176.

Harcourt, who took the Fenian threat more seriously than his colleagues and whom she had described 10 months previously as "the only Minister of the present Government that had any determination", though he was to recover his stock with her when he forced the Prevention of Crimes (Ireland) Act through Parliament between May and July in 1882.[154] Granville tried to placate her by pointing to the advantage of having Maclean's act speedily determined to be that of madman, and Harcourt by pointing out that had a death sentence been imposed it would probably have been commuted and then attempts would have been made to secure a further commutation.[155]

There was one paper, *The Englishman*, which also saw governmental collusion in the affair but insinuated that Victoria herself was part of it. She had at last found a wife for her youngest son, Leopold,[156] and at the end of March she transmitted to Parliament the address that was customary in such circumstances. It asked Parliament to increase Leopold's Civil List annuity to enable him to support his enlarged household and to provide a pension for his bride in the event of her becoming widowed. The grant was, as often,[157] opposed, especially as it was extremely unlikely that heirs to the throne would have to be sought in the line of descent

---

154. Gardner, *supra* n. 82, at p. 429 and 440-452; Porter, 1987, *supra* n. 39, at 38.
155. Letters from Granville to the Queen, (Apr. 20, 1882) and from Ponsonby to the Queen, (Apr. 20, 1882), RA L14/138 and 139. See too the remarks of Lord Coleridge conveyed to Ponsonby through Lindsay, Letter from Lindsay to Ponsonby, (Apr. 19, 1882), RA L14/137.
156. "It suddenly struck me that he should go and look at the Princess Helen of Waldeck", Longford, *supra* n. 32a, at. 561.
157. Hardie, *supra* n. 47, at 207 and 218.

from Leopold, and an opposition led by Henry Labouchere, Timothy Healy, and Henry Broadhurst divided the Commons on the issue.[158] *The Englishman* suggested that the whole Maclean affair had been stage managed from the start so that the Leopold grant would be carried through on a wave of sympathy for Victoria.[159] The Duke of Albany (Establishment) Bill completed its passage through Parliament on the day after Maclean's trial and received the Royal Assent the same day. Within two years, Leopold, who was haemophiliac, was dead and his widow in receipt of her pension.

Gladstone's response to the Queen was virtually an admission that the Government had connived at the special verdict in a case where it was not justified:

> "Mr Gladstone humbly feels with your Majesty that when an individual such as Maclean, *has probably been sane in respect to the particular act for which he is tried*, an acquittal on the ground of insanity is not a satisfactory form under which to attain the end of at least disabling him from further mischief by the total loss of his personal liberty." [my emphasis].

---

158. 267 Parl. Deb., HC (ser. 3) 1703 (1882). The debate on the grant raised the intriguing constitutional issue of whether members of Parliament, during the reading of an Address from the Crown, should take their hats off. It transpired that the Rule was that they should if, as in the case of the request for the grant to Leopold, it was one initiated by the Crown but that they need not when it was a response to an Address by them to the monarch. So it had been in order for them to remain covered when Victoria's message of thanks for their Address on her escape from Maclean had been read to them, 267 Parl. Deb., HC (ser.3) 141 (1882).
159. *The Englishman* (London), Mar. 11, 1882, at 305, Apr. 4, 1882, at 369, and Apr. 22, 1882 at 401.

But at the same time he contended that in the particular case the Government could not have done otherwise and that therefore the best course had been followed. He undertook, however, to have the possibility of a change in the form of the verdict examined.[160]

Shortly afterwards, Gladstone and James met with Coleridge to canvass the alteration of the form of the verdict. It was agreed that the advice of the "most competent and learned judges" would be taken. Coleridge did not commit himself to any view but apparently thought that, while it would be difficult to change the law in relation to murder, a change in relation to treason might be possible.[161] There was historical precedent for excluding treason from the scope of the insanity defence[162] and the idea of a revival of some form of this may not have come first from Coleridge. The memorandum written by James on Maclean's trial contained the observation that

> "It is suggested by some writers on very doubtful grounds that in remote times insane persons could be convicted of High Treason. For centuries certainly this view has not prevailed - and at common law a person found to be

---

160. Letter from Gladstone to the Queen, (Apr. 20, 1882), reprinted in 2 Guedalla, *supra* n. 17, at 186[855]. Only the first part of this letter is reprinted in 3 Bucke, *supra* n. 16, at 269.

161. Letter from Gladstone to the Queen, (May 3, 1882), reprinted in 3 Buckle, *supra* n. 16, at 278. Only the first part of this letter is printed in 2 Guedalla, *supra* n. 17, at 188[857].

162. Moran's statement, *supra* n. 1, at 176, that the Treason Act, 1541, 32 Hen. VIII, ch. 2 "eliminat[ed] the defence of insanity for attempting to assassinate the sovereign" is a little misleading. The statute dealt only with those who appeared to become insane after being tried.

insane at the time of the committal of any offence was entitled to a verdict of acquittal."[163]

In the event Coleridge consulted Bowen and Fitzjames Stephen JJ about the desirability of "making some alteration in the trials of insane persons guilty of attacks upon the Queen".[164] When Ponsonby was informed of developments shortly after he noted that the judges were going to be consulted about a change in the form of the verdict in cases of "shooting at the Queen".[165]

Coleridge sent the judges' report to Gladstone towards the end of the month. It has not been located but a minute in Gladstone's papers records:

"Lord Chief Justice Coleridge sends report from himself and Mr Justice Stephen and Bowen upon verdicts for Treason. As lawyers think a verdict of guilty qualified by

---

163. Memorandum, (Apr. 20, 1882), Gladstone Papers, vol. 134, f. 61, Add 44,219. The memorandum was duplicated as a briefing document for Harcourt's attendance on the Queen, Ms. Harcourt dep. 96, at f. 71, but, as has been seen, she declined to see him.

164. Letter from James to Gladstone, (May 13, 1882), Gladstone Papers, v. 134, f. 63, Add. 44,219. In February the following year Stephen sent Gladstone a copy of his *History of the Criminal Law of England* and referred him to the chapters on mental disorder and crime, commenting "It contains my views on the subject you may remember consulting Lord Coleridge, Lord Justice Bowen and myself last summer". Letter from Stephen to Gladstone, (Feb. 1, 1883), Gladstone Papers, v. 394, f. 190, Add. 44,479. For Gladstone's reply, (Feb. 6, 1883), Gladstone Papers, v. 461, f. 77, Add. 44,546 reprinted in Matthew, *supra* n. 37, at 403.

165. Minute by Ponsonby on Gladstone's letter to him, (May 15, 1882), RA L14/141a. Unfortunately I have not been able to find a copy of the note from the Attorney-General which accompanied it.

additional reference to mental condition of prisoner, might be added. Express no opinion on political consequences of such a verdict."[166]

By September, it seems, the alteration to be made had been agreed upon[167] and towards the end of the year it had been decided to include an amending provision in a forthcoming Criminal Law Consolidation Bill.[168] This was one of several attempts made almost annually between 1879 and 1883 to codify criminal law and procedure. The new provision first appeared as clause 107 of the Criminal Code (Indictable Offences Procedure) Bill, 1883.[169] It provided for a special verdict of "guilty but insane" in any trial by jury, not just in cases of treason as at one time it seemed it might have. The verdict was to be returned:

> "Where any act or omission is charged against any person as an offence, and it is given in evidence on the trial of such person for that offence that he was insane, so as not to be responsible for his actions ..., [and] it appears to the jury before whom such person is tried that he did nor made the act or omission charged, but was insane as aforesaid ..."

Although given a first reading in February, the bill's progress

166. Minute, (May 29, 1882), Gladstone Papers, v. 53, f. 233, Add. 44,219.
167. Note by Ponsonby, (Aug.21, 1883), RA L15/15.
168. Letter from Gladstone to Ponsonby, (Nov. 29, 1882), RA L15/24. With this letter Gladstone enclosed a memorandum on the proposed change from Law Officers - but it has not been located.
169. HC Bill 8.

was controversial and slow and in June the Standing Committee on Law, Courts of Justice and Legal Procedure, to which it had been referred, having considered only eight of the 131 clauses, reported that it had decided to proceed no further with the bill as it would be impossible to make sufficient progress with it in the time available.[170] The provision relating to the special verdict was thereupon extracted from it and made the subject of a separate bill,[171] which was passed with minor amendments quickly and quietly in August at the end of the Parliamentary session.[172] The explanation given by James to the House of Commons was that the altered verdict would have a deterrent effect on those contemplating the commission of a crime when only partially mad[173] and the emphasis on those "not completely responsible" was repeated in his memorandum on the Act which Gladstone sent to Victoria.[174]

Victoria was well pleased with the measure and pained Gladstone by singling it out from all the Acts passed in the session as a cause for satisfaction.[175]

---

170. *Special Report and Reports on the Criminal Code (Indictable Offences Procedure) Bill and the Court of Criminal Appeal Bill with the Proceedings of the Standing Committee on Law and Courts of Justice and Legal Procedure*, June 26, 1883, HC Paper 225; and HC Jour., June 26, 1883, at 301.
171. Letter from Gladstone to the Queen, (Aug, 2, 1882), RA A58/71.
172. For the Lords' amendments see HL Jour. Aug. 9 and 13, 1883. The amendment made by the Commons is apparent from HC Bill 292.
173. 283 Parl. Deb., HC (ser.3) 922 (1882).
174. Letter from Gladstone to the Queen, Aug. 20, 1883, reprinted in Walker, *supra* n. 44, at 191. James's Memorandum, Aug. 20, 1883, is at RA L15/14.
175. Letter from the Queen to Gladstone, (Aug. 23, 1883) reprinted in 3 Buckle, *supra* n. 16, 438; 2 Ballman, *supra* n. 37, 475.

Contemporary Significance

As has been seen, immediately after the Act came into force the courts had some difficulty in determining what exactly was meant by "the act charged as an offence".[176] There is evidence from around the country that courts today are being exercised by the same problem when embarking on a "trial of the facts" under the Criminal Procedure (Insanity and Unfitness to Plead) Act, 1991.[177] After the establishment of the Court of Criminal Appeal the court had to decide whether the special verdict, having become one of "guilty," amounted to a conviction against which an appeal was allowed by the Criminal Appeal Act:[178] the House of Lords eventually decided that it did not, and an appeal against it was not provided until the Criminal Procedure (Insanity) Act of 1964. More recently a question was raised for the first time about whether the effect of the 1883 Act is to prevent insanity

---

176. See *supra* p.4.
177. On this Act see White, "The Criminal Procedure (Insanity and Unfitness to Plead) Act 1991", [1992] *Criminal Law Review* 4; Fennell, "The Criminal Procedure (Insanity and Unfitness to Plead) Act 1991", 55 *Modern Law Review* 547 (1992); Dolan and Campbell, "The Criminal Procedure (Insanity and Unfitness to Plead) Act, 1991: A Case Report and Selected Review of the Legal Reforms", 34 *Medicine Science and the Law* 155 (1994); Mackay and Kearns, "The Continued Underuse of Unfitness to Plead and the Insanity Defence", [1994] *Criminal Law Review* 576; Cripps and James, "An Insane Way to Behave? Sources of Confusion under the Criminal Procedure (Insanity and Unfitness to Plead) Act 1991", 6 *Journal of Forensic Psychiatry* 606 (1995); Mackay and Kearns, "The Trial of Facts and Unfitness to Plead", [1997] *Criminal Law Review* 644; White, "Acts and Facts", 62 *Journal of Criminal Law* 360 (1998).
178. *R. v. Ireland* [1910] 1 KB 54; *R. v. Machardy* [1911] 2 KB 1144; *R. v. Hill* 7 Cr. App. R. 26 and 83 (1911); *R. v. Felstead* [1914] AC 534; *R. v. Taylor* [1915] 2 KB 709.

defences being entertained by magistrates' courts[179] for the Act provides that

> "where in any indictment or *information* any act or omission is charged against any person as an offence ... if it appears to the *jury* ... that he did the act or made the omission charged, but was insane ... the *jury shall* return" (my emphasis)

the special verdict. Since these days juries do not try informations it was widely thought that the effect of the Act was to oblige magistrates to commit for trial whenever a defence of insanity was in the offing so that a jury might pronounce upon it, at least if they were not able to dispose of the case by using their powers under s.37(3) of the Mental Health Act, 1983.[180]

An opposing view was that when the Act was passed juries did try certain sorts of information and that it was to these informations only that the Act is referring. In 1883 criminal proceedings by way of information could be initiated in the High Court either by the Master of the Crown Office on behalf of a private individual[181] or *ex officio* by the

---

179. White, "Sullivan's Choice", 148 *Justice of the Peace* 318 (1984) and White, "Insanity in a Magistrates' Court", 148 *Justice of the Peace* 419, 435 and 452 (1984). See to White, "Insanity Defences in Magistrates' Courts", [1991] *Criminal Law Review* 501.

180. Crosta, "Sullivan's Choice", 144 *Justice of the Peace* 245 (1984) and Crosta, "Insanity in a Magistrates' Court - A Reply", 148 *Justice of the Peace* 557 (1984).

181. Abolished by Administration of Justice Act, 1938, 1 and 2 Geo. 6, ch. 61, s.12.

Attorney General:[182] the prosecution of Parnell, for example, was on an *ex officio* information.[183] Unfortunately three memoranda which might shed light on whether the Act was intended to apply to summary trials have not been discovered[184] but the chronology of the passing of the Act makes it probable that it was not.

The phrase "in any indictment or information" did not appear in clause 107 of the Criminal Code (Indictable Offences Procedure) Bill. On 9, 10, and 11 May 1883 two proceedings concerning informations were conducted in the Queen's Bench Division. Both involved prosecutions for libel. In one, leave was sought to file an information against Labouchere, the editor of *Truth*, for libelling the Duke of Vallombrosa, a dead foreign aristocrat.[185] In the other, Edmund Yates, the editor of *The World*, sought to quash an information which had been filed against him with the leave of the court. In neither case had the consent of the Director of Public Prosecutions been obtained and it was argued in the former case that the information should not be issued, and in the latter that it should be quashed, because s.3 of the Newspaper Libel and Registrations Act, 1881, prohibited any "criminal prosecution" being started against a newspaper proprietor without the Director's consent. Sir Henry James appeared to oppose the application in *Yates* and argued that,

---

182. Abolished by Criminal Law Act 1967, s. 6(6).
183. *Supra* p. 18.
184. James's note which accompanied Gladstone's letter to Ponsonby, the judges' report, and the Law Officers' memorandum on the proposed change. In addition to the sources already mentioned the James papers at the Hereford Record Office (MS 45) have also been searched.
185. *R. v. Labouchere* [1884] 12 QBD 320.

although unqualified, the words "criminal prosecution" did not apply to prosecutions by way of information. On July 3 the court delivered its decision and by a majority of three to two agreed with him.[186] In the judgments every type of prosecution is examined in order to determine whether it is or is not a "criminal prosecution" for the purposes of the 1881 Act, Field J commenting that the difficulty of the case arose from "the use by the legislature of general and what may almost be called popular language instead of precise words, the well known import and effect of which when used leave no room for doubt as to their meaning". Here surely lies the explanation for the appearance of the phrase "in any indictment or information" in the Trial of Lunatics Bill when it was introduced on 2 August 1883. The precedent "any indictment or information" can be found in the Libel Acts of 1792 and 1843, which were passed when prosecutions for libel had to be brought by way of information in the High Court, as they did in 1883.[187] Lord Brett, MR, was to say in the following year, when Yates appealed unsuccessfully to the Court of Appeal,

> "It was also argued that the phrase 'criminal prosecution' was one ordinarily used by lawyers to express that which would comprise both a prosecution by indictment and a criminal information. So far from agreeing to that, I think, according to my experience, that this is the very phrase

---

186. *The Queen on the Prosecution of the Earl of Lonsdale v. Yates* 11 QBD 750 (1883).
187. See Spencer, "Criminal Libel", [1992] *Criminal Law Review* 383 and Spencer, "The Press and the Reform of Criminal Libel" in *Reshaping the Criminal Law; Essays in Honour of Glanville Williams* (P. Glazebrook ed. 1978), 266.

> they would not use, and that by a criminal prosecution for libel they would mean a prosecution by indictment or before a magistrate, as distinguished from a proceeding by criminal information".[188]

This account of the effect of the word "information" in the section has recently been accepted by the Divisional Court, which has made it clear that the common law relating to insanity defences, untouched by statute, applies in magistrates' courts.[189] Magistrates can entertain such defences and the outcome of a successful defence is an unqualified acquittal and the unconditional liberation of the defendant unless a hospital order under Mental Health Act 1983 s.37(3) can be made. Section 37(3), however, is not linked to the insanity defence as the powers of the courts under the Trial of Lunatics Act and the Criminal Procedure (Insanity and Unfitness to Plead) Act are. Section 37(3) will apply to some, but not all, defendants who were insane at the time of their alleged offences, and it will apply to many who were not.

---

188. *Yates v. The Queen* 14 QBD 648 at 655 (1884).
189. *R. v. Horseferry Road Magistrates' Court, ex parte K* [1996] 3 All ER 719 and *D.P.P. v. Harper* [1997] 1 WLR 1406; 38 BMLR 91; [1997] RTR 200. See too White and Bowen, "Insanity Defences in Summary Trials", 61 *Journal of Criminal Law* 198 (1997) and Ward, "Magistrates, Insanity and the Common Law", [1997] *Criminal Law Review* 796.

Conclusion

The is still something about the passage of the 1883 Act that is puzzling. Victoria had been forewarned of the path Maclean's trial was likely to take and what the prosecution's strategy was to be. She had noted them in her Journal uncomplainingly. Yet her reaction to the verdict was a surprised outrage sufficient to persuade the Government that it should comply, against its better judgment, with her wish for the law to be changed.

The explanation, it is tentatively suggested, lies in a combination of two factors: the significance for Victoria of April 19, the day of Maclean's trial, and further developments in Ireland immediately afterwards. Within a fortnight of Maclean's trial Parnell had been released from Kilmainham gaol, and Forster, Gladstone's Irish Secretary, has resigned. Victoria had protested to Gladstone at the release and predicted that it would be "very hazardous".[190] Three days later Lord Frederick Cavendish, Foster's replacement, had been stabbed to death by the Invincibles in Phoenix Park.[191] As well as being a political catastrophe this was a devastating personal blow for Gladstone. Cavendish was related by marriage to him and he had treated Cavendish as a favourite son. Victoria restrained

190. Letter from the Queen to Gladstone, (May 3, 1882), reprinted in 3 Buckle, *supra* n. 16, at 277. All but the first introductory paragraph is printed in 2 Guedalla, *supra* n. 17, at 188[858].

191. See sources cited *supra* n.37. A piece applauding the murders in similar vein to that hailing the assassination of the Tsar led to a second prosecution against a couple of the *Der Freiheit's* compositors and its being closed down, see sources cited *supra* n. 39.

herself from saying "I told you so"[192] to Gladstone but to Granville she wrote (her emphasis)

> "While the Queen does not wish to pain Lord Granville at this moment ... she *cannot withhold* from him that *she* considers this horrible event the direct result of what she has always considered and has stated to Mr. Gladstone and to Lord Spencer as a most fatal and hazardous step ...
>
> Mr Forster's words were prophetic, spoken only two days before; that this unconditional release of these dangerous men was 'an encouragement to crime'. *How* right he was, last night's fearful occurrence has only proved too well.
>
> The Queen now deeply regrets that before giving her assent - which was almost extorted from her - she did not say she wished for 24 hour's reflection; ...
>
> What Mr Gladstone's feelings must be under the circumstances can be imagined."[193]

Granville told Ponsonby that were he to show the letter to the Cabinet they would have no option but to resign.[194]

As for April 19, the day of Maclean's trial was always going to be a sorrowful one for Victoria because it was the first anniversary of Disraeli's (Lord Beaconsfield's) death. In the year before his death she had sent him a Valentine, and

---

192. Letter from the Queen to Gladstone, (May 9, 1882), reprinted in 3 Buckle, *supra* n. 16, at 292, and in 2 Guedalla, *supra* n. 17, at 194[865].
193. Letter from the Queen to Earl Granville, (May 7, 1882), reprinted in 3 Buckle, *supra* n. 16, at 284.
194. Granville to Ponsonby, in Ponsonby *supra* n. 32a, at 191.

the memorial tablet she placed in Hughenden Church[195] bore an inscription from *Proverbs*, 16, 13: "Kings love him that speaketh right". She had been so overwhelmed by his death as to pen the notice of it in the Court Circular personally and to drop the royal third person singular when writing a letter of condolence to Disraeli's private secretary. Etiquette preventing her attending his funeral, she had had Disraeli's family vault at Hughenden reopened four days later so that she could visit his tomb. To the funeral itself she had sent two wreaths of primroses with the message, "His favourite flowers from Osborne, a tribute of affection from Queen Victoria".[196]

Five days before Maclean's trial a correspondence to *The Times* reported the demand for "Beaconsfield buttonholes", and bouquets of primroses had spangled the laps of the packed court at Reading.[197] It is to these primroses that we should look in part for an explanation of the Trial of Lunatics Act, 1883. They certainly intimate the full import of Herbert Stephen's remark that the Act "would not have been passed if the occurrence which led to it had taken place during the Premiership of Lord Beaconsfield".

---

195. *Supra* n. 101.
196. Some thought that the "his" referred to the Prince Consort who had died twenty years before, R. Blake, *Disraeli*, 703 and 749-753 (1966); Longford, *supra* n. 32a, at p. 548; G. Buckle, *The Life of Benjamin Disraeli Earl of Beaconsfield, Vol. VI 1876-1881*, 618-623 (1920).
197. *The Times* (London), Apr. 14, 1882, at 7, col. e; Buckle, *supra* n. 196, at pp. 628-632; 10 *Students' Journal and Hospital Gazette* 175 (Apr. 29, 1882).

Index

(The letter "n" immediately following a page reference, indicates a relevant footnote on that page)